Robert Kelly SJ

GIVE GOD A CHANCE

How to let God take charge of your life

VERITAS

Published 1993 by
Veritas Publications
7-8 Lower Abbey Street
Dublin 1

ISBN 1 85390 276 4

British Library Cataloguing
in Publication Data.
A catalogue record for
this book is available
from the British Library.

Scripture quotations are taken from the *Jerusalem Bible*, published and copyright 1966, 1967 and 1968 by Darton, Longman & Todd Ltd and Doubleday, a division of Bantam, Doubleday, Dell Publishing Group, Inc., and are used by permission of the publishers.

Cover design by Joseph Gervin
Printed in the Republic of Ireland
by The Leinster Leader

CONTENTS

INTRODUCTION

Always have your answer ready for people who
ask you the reason for the hope that you have.
1 Peter 3:15

With these words St Peter encourages his fellow Christians
to be ready to explain to others why they follow the new
Christian way of life, why they have accepted Jesus Christ
and believe in him. His words apply to believers of all
times, to you and me today. If our Christian faith has real
meaning for us, we should be ready to explain to others
who may ask us why we believe and live as we do.

As life goes on, the most important questioner I must be
ready to explain my religious hope to is myself. The most
important questions to be answered are the ones I ask
myself when I am alone. What does Jesus Christ mean to
me? Why do I believe in him and try to follow him? What
difference does he make to my life? If I cannot answer
these questions to my own self, I am unlikely to be able to
explain my Christian hope to others.

Let us notice the kind of questions we are speaking
about here. We are not concerned so much with intellectual questions and answers. We are not talking about scor-
ing high marks in a Christian doctrine exam. Many of us
would feel intimidated by such an exam. Recent years
have seen rapid and startling changes in our world. It is
very obvious in the area of technology, but it is happening
with equal speed and force in the world of ideas, culture,
religious beliefs. One of my favourite comic postcards
shows a picture of a bewildered teddy-bear poring over a
large book with a caption which says, 'There has been an
alarming increase in the number of things I know nothing
about!' We can be intimidated by the development of sci-
ence, technology and new skills in our secular world. Now,
our faith life, our religious beliefs and practices are subject
to their own growth process and development. As a result,

many good Christians feel less confident about explaining or defending their Christian beliefs. Startled by new interpretations of traditional faith, they feel less secure.

Thus it may seem harder than ever in our time to respond to Peter's urging that we should be ready to explain our Christian hope to those who ask. But the Christian message, the Good News, is more about salvation than about having correct answers to difficult doctrinal questions or providing neat solutions to the complex problems of life. The heart and centre of our faith is a person, Jesus Christ, and this person, Jesus, offers a salvation that may be deeply experienced, just at a time when correct doctrinal answers elude us.

If we were to ask Peter himself to explain the hope he had, I am sure he would start to speak of Jesus Christ, how he met him and how life was never the same again. And Peter understands that this Jesus is at the centre of the lives of the Christians he is writing to. To them he writes, 'You did not see Jesus, yet you love him; and still without seeing him, you are filled with a joy so glorious that it cannot be described, because you believe.' This book offers some reflections which may help us to share the experience of those early Christians who, like us, did not see the Lord but loved him. That love was real for them. Indeed it was the greatest reality in their lives and filled them with a joy so glorious that it was difficult to describe.

1 Pet
1:8 9

1

ANNO DOMINI

In identifying dates in history, we use the letters BC to indicate the years before the birth of Christ. We identify all subsequent years by the letters AD, which stand for *Anno Domini*, the year of the Lord. Notice that we do not refer to those years as AC, after Christ. This is perhaps the most startling claim our faith makes. It is the basis of all our hope, namely that there is no such thing as time after Christ. Jesus Christ is alive today. We live in his time.

For a Christian believer there are only two periods of history, the time before Christ and the time of Christ. But often, by the way we speak and act, we Christians seem to suggest that there are three periods of history: the time before Christ, described in the Old Testament; the time of Christ, as described in the New Testament; and the time after Christ, which is the rest of history and, for us, today, is this modern age. This way of thinking leads to greatly reduced expectations of our faith. It encourages us to accept a very watered-down version of our Christian hope. It deprives us of power and spiritual nourishment. The Good News of our faith is that we live in the time of Jesus Christ. He is alive and among us. We can meet him and have his friendship. He is doing or wants to do among us what he did when he entered our world in the incarnation.

The Good News of our faith is eternally modern. It is a 'today' thing. It is always a 'now' event. It is happening. It is Good News. It is not a 'history' of good things that God did in former days. It is not a 'prophecy' of things God will do in future when we become more worthy of his love. No! It is what God is doing or wants to do for us right now. It is 'news'. When we open the daily newspaper, we expect to read about what is happening right now in the world about us. We would not accept last week's newspaper from our newsagent. The gospel message is not only news, it is good news telling us about God's presence and activity here and now in our lives. This activity is re-creating, healing and liberating. The message of the good news is spoken afresh all the time and is addressed to me by name. I am not a spectator of revealed truth being handed to someone else and passed on to me. I am the addressee. The message is spoken to my heart and if I listen with faith, the words become reality in my life. After Jesus announced the good news in the synagogue of Nazareth, he looked at his audience and said, 'This text is being fulfilled today even as you listen' (Luke 4:22).

The words that God speaks to us through Jesus are different from all other words. Scripture calls them 'living words'. These living words, which are as fresh and alive as God himself in every age, reveal God's very inner being which is love. The Bible is not a book of information about God aimed at my intellect. It is the self-revelation of God's heart aimed at my heart. The word is 'I love you'. Faith is not a matter of looking for correct intellectual answers to difficult questions about the existence and nature of God. Faith involves my answer to the one, all-important question which he puts to me: Do you love me? It was the question put to Peter at the lakeside of Tiberias after the resurrection (John 21:15).

This very question put to us by God brings us into a world of wonder and mystery. It tells us we are 'the sought-after' (Isaiah 62:12). God seeks our love. We think of St Augustine's words, 'You have made us for yourself, O Lord, and our hearts are restless until they rest in you.' It has been so from the beginning. The first book of the Bible describes God walking in the garden with the first man and woman. He strolls with them in the evening, chatting as friend with friend. Then the dialogue is interrupted. Something goes wrong. Evil is present. Sin follows. The conversation breaks down. God's friends experience shame, fear and guilt, and they hide. God, their friend, is not happy. He wants the friendship to continue and searches for his friends. 'Adam, where are you?' (Genesis 3:9) – and the answer comes, 'I was afraid because I was naked, so I hid.'

God did not give up on his friends. He continued to search for them, to search for us. He sent message after message through many prophets, through many years. Through these years the guilt increased. When misfortune came, people saw it as God's revenge and anger and they cried out, 'Yahweh has abandoned me, the Lord has forgotten me' (Isaiah 49:14). They are far away from knowing the mystery of God's love. Yahweh answered their cry:

> Does a woman forget her baby at the breast
> or fail to cherish the son of her womb?
> Yet even if these forget,
> I will never forget you.
> *Isaiah 49:15*

Despite this beautiful word, fear still held sway. Guilt erected great barriers, terrible walls. And the fear and guilt were reinforced by false teachers, self-righteous people who felt sure they knew what God was like. These teachers told people that they were outcasts and that their sickness and misfortune were punishments from an angry God. Such teaching was a great dark cloud obscuring the sunshine of God's love.

What can God do? He seeks us and wants to convince our hearts of his love. He has spoken many words of love through the prophets. What more can he do? He will speak one more word, his greatest and clearest word. But now he will take no more chances. He will not rely on spoken words which can be misunderstood and misinterpreted. He will send his Son, he will send his word in the flesh. 'The Word was made flesh, he lived among us' (John 1:14). The bright warm sunshine of God's love broke through that dark cloud of guilt, fear and false teaching and shone upon us. The love of God became visible in Jesus. God

9

would once again walk on earth and talk with his friends, man and woman, and he does not seem to mind that they are labelled 'sinners' by the self-righteous. He is happy to be called 'friend of sinners'. We are still 'the sought-after', even in our sins.

'At various times in the past and in various different ways, God spoke to our ancestors through the prophets; but in our own time, the last days, he has spoken to us through his Son' (Hebrews 1:1-2). Notice 'in our own time'. Jesus speaks now. It is Paul's time, it is Peter's time, it is our time, *anno domini*. He speaks to me, to us, today. We know from the gospel the extraordinary power of the words of Jesus. People hung on his words. They forgot about food as they followed him out into the desert to listen to him. They said, 'There has never been anybody who has spoken like him' (John 7:46). These words have not lost their power as they are spoken afresh to us today. His teaching was different from that of the scribes and Pharisees. 'His teaching made a deep impression on them because, unlike the scribes, he taught them with authority' (Mark 1:22).

Jesus speaks with authority. Let us understand this well. There is deep meaning in this word 'authority' which we could miss, quite different from our ordinary understanding. The authority with which Jesus speaks is not something external to the word he speaks. Jesus is not saying 'I am your new religious teacher and you must listen and believe because I say it.' He is not even saying, 'I am the Son of God and so you must accept my word.' Something more wonderful is happening. The authority is in the very word itself. He speaks the Truth. The Truth needs no authority outside of itself to command obedience. When the people hear the word of Jesus, it touches the deepest part of themselves, the heart and centre of each person made in God's image. His word reaches that deep centre and, wonderful to relate, an echo comes back from that deep place, an echo which agrees and says Amen.

Here lies the power of Truth, its nourishing and trans-
forming power. We are made for Truth. The word of Jesus
is the Truth. Jesus himself, the word made flesh, is the
Truth. Our deepest good self, made in God's image, hears,
'knows' and responds to this Truth which is Jesus. He himself said that his followers know his voice. 'The sheep hear
his voice, one by one he calls his own sheep. He goes
ahead of them and the sheep follow because they know his
voice' (John 10:3-4). Jesus speaks our name in love and our
deepest self recognises him and his word. Maybe we cannot describe this exactly to others, but we 'know' that
something beautiful and mysterious is happening. St Paul
speaks of this. Writing to the Christians in Rome he
reminds them that they have not received a spirit of fear
but the spirit of children, 'and it makes us cry out "Abba,
Father!" The Spirit himself and our spirit bear united witness that we are children of God' (Romans 8:14-16). Notice
what he says: 'the Spirit himself and our spirit bear united
witness.' That is, when God's spirit tells us we are his children, our own spirit recognises the truth, there is an echo
from our deepest self. This deep self accepts and is moved
to 'cry out, "Abba, Father"'.

Something like this was happening when Jesus looked
around at the crowd and told them that God loved them as
children. That's why they forgot about food to listen to
him. They were hungry for this truth. When he told them
they were children of the Father, that they were more
beautiful than the flowers; when he told them that their
Father loved them even as he loved Jesus himself; when he
told them their sins were forgiven and their sickness was
not sent by God as punishment, they knew they were
hearing the truth and they were transformed.

We live in his time. It is today. It is our time. We need not
envy the first Christians. He is with us to the end of time
as Friend and Saviour. He invites us to accept his friendship and salvation. He wants to speak his word to us
today, the word of truth which can nourish and transform

us. He would like us to talk to him, to share ourselves with him, to tell him the story of our life. And he would like us to listen to him and let him share himself with us and tell us his story, what it was like for him to live out a truly human life among us. As we listen he will share the secrets of his Father with us. He will lead us into the mystery and wonder of his Father's being and into the mystery and wonder of our own being. He will lead us to the truth about God, about himself and about our own selves. This truth can touch the deepest part of us and release unexpected springs of life, growth and beauty. The wasteland within us can bloom again. Our dry hearts can become a beautiful garden for God where he will be pleased to walk, as he walked in the original garden of creation with the first man and woman.

2

FROM BELIEVING TO KNOWING

On one occasion towards the end of his life, St Paul is in prison in Caesarea awaiting transfer to Rome for trial. The governor, Festus, is explaining to a visitor, King Agrippa, the curious charges being brought against Paul. 'His accusers did not charge him with any of the crimes I had expected; but they had some argument or other with him... about a dead man called Jesus whom Paul alleged to be alive' (Acts 25:18-19). For Festus and Paul's enemies, Jesus was a 'dead man', no more. But for Paul and the Christian believers, Jesus is alive and among them, their living Lord and Friend whom they can know and love and for whom they are joyfully prepared to die.

So for us Christians today, Jesus is alive and with us. We not only believe in him, we can know him, have personal friendship with him and experience this friendship as the source of our deepest joy and power. Peter's words to the first believers should apply to us. 'You did not see him, yet you love him; and still without seeing him, you are already filled with a joy so glorious that it cannot be described, because you believe' (1 Peter 1:8-9). Our faith must touch the whole person and not just the mind only. The risen, present Lord offers his love to our hearts. After the crucifixion of Jesus, two of his disillusioned disciples are on the road to Emmaus, certain that their Jesus was a dead man. But then he joins them on the road and their eyes are opened. This is how they described their experience. 'Did not our hearts burn within us as he talked to us on the road' (Luke 24:32). Believing should lead to knowing and knowing must touch the heart.

We live in *anno domini*. We believe that Jesus is risen, alive and with us as we journey on the road of life. Yet many do not seem to experience his presence warming their hearts. Hopefully, it is not that they think that Jesus is

13

a dead man. But many would say that for them he is distant and not so 'real', not as real as family or friends, or as real as the daily cares and problems, or the joyful recreations that make life happier. Believing in Jesus does not bring the 'glorious joy' of which Peter speaks. The duties of Christian life often seem irksome. Prayer, charity, parish involvement and communal worship are mostly seen as 'duties', activities imposed by outside authorities rather than a real experience of something going on within the person, a friendship with the living Lord deep within, which should provide the inspiration, joy and power to enable us to follow him. Often, believing does not lead to this 'knowing' experience.

I wonder why this is so. Why do so many stop at believing, and have only a kind of intellectual relationship with Jesus? Why do so few progress to knowing the Lord personally and to enjoying a heart experience? I suggest it has something to do with the way they are introduced to Jesus. Many Christians first meet Jesus in a catechism or creed rather than in the gospel story. They meet Jesus as true God in the Creed and have little experience of him as true man in the gospel. And most who meet Jesus in this way were introduced to him in a school setting, in a Christian doctrine class. This relatively dry and shallow encounter seldom progresses to a deeper, more personal relationship.

From classroom they progressed to Christian practice in a parish community where faith was meant to be nourished chiefly by attendance at Church devotions and services. This attendance was often motivated by a spirit of conformity rather than any deep personal conviction. This is an over-simplification, but many readers will agree that it reflects their general experience. This road of faith led many good, devout people to lives of great fidelity and true holiness. But, for today, faith will have to be more personally experienced if it is to meet the challenges of our time. And Christ wishes us to have this experience. He came that we might have life and have it to the full. He

14

wishes to reveal himself to us and lead us to joy in knowing him. How might this happen?

Let us look at those Christians Peter writes to in the letter we have quoted. Like us they did not see the Lord in the flesh. They met him in faith by believing. Peter observes that this faith knowledge led to love and this love filled them with a joy so glorious it was hard to describe. How were those believers introduced to Jesus? We might say they had an advantage over us since they were introduced to Jesus by the very first followers who had known him in the flesh. But we have to remember that even those first followers who had known Jesus in the flesh had to progress to a faith relationship with him. Not all who met Jesus in the flesh accepted him or believed in him. He had his enemies. Not all who were attracted to him followed him. We think of the rich young man. And some who started as disciples fell away when he proposed teachings they could not accept. When he said he would give himself as food and drink, we are told, 'After this, many of his disciples left him and stopped going with him' (John 6:66).

I suggest it can help if we go back to those very first followers and recall their experience of meeting the Lord and how they handed on that experience to those Christians Peter is writing to. I think this will help us believers of today to achieve a closer affinity with our first brothers and sisters in the faith and to a more personal experience of Jesus in our own faith lives. The very first followers did not meet Jesus in a creed. They met a man of flesh and blood. John writes: 'Something . . . that we have heard, and we have seen with our own eyes; that we have watched and touched with our hands: the Word who is life – this is our subject' (1 John 1:1). This Jesus they met was an unusual man who, by his words and lifestyle, provoked many questions. 'Whatever kind of man is this? Even the winds and the sea obey him' (Matthew 8:27). 'What authority have you for acting like this?' (Matthew 21:23). 'Why does he eat with sinners?' (Mark 2:16). 'How did he

NB

learn to read? He has not been taught' (John 7:15). 'Who are you claiming to be?' (John 8:54). Some who met this strange man and listened to him were deeply attracted. They became his disciples, ready to learn more and adopt his lifestyle. Of course they had lots of unanswered questions, plenty of wrong ideas and false hopes. But in time they would learn the deeper reality and meaning of this strange and fascinating man.

This deeper understanding came, paradoxically, through the totally unexpected trauma of Jesus' suffering and death. This tragedy devastated his disciples. It appeared to be total catastrophe and it came very quickly, within a matter of a few years. Their master, their hero who had made claims which sounded as if he was invulnerable, suddenly broke down completely. One night he went to pieces before their very eyes. He was forcibly taken prisoner, was rejected by the people, apparently abandoned by God and handed over to a colonial government. He was tortured and crucified. All their hopes were dead, as dead as the corpse they laid in the tomb.

Then came something totally new, resurrection from the dead. These first followers meet Jesus again. They are slow at first to recognise and believe it was really he. Gradually the truth dawns on them. He is alive. He is risen from the dead. He is the same Jesus they had known and lived with. He is the same and yet in some way different. He is the same gentle, compassionate, loving person, but there is some strange new quality about him. And now a new relationship blossoms, a deeper awareness is reached about their master and friend, a deeper understanding of his relationship with God. He is the Messiah, but no mere prophet, he truly is the Beloved Son of God.

They have met and known the man, but have now come to know that he is the Son of God. And this Son of God, who called them friends, has brought their humanity into a new and glorified existence where they are to follow. Once they had accepted this great mystery, that the one they had known as a man was truly God, they became transformed people and began to see the true meaning of everything. Their own lives now took on an incredibly new and beautiful depth. Their humble lives are suffused with extraordinary meaning and beauty. These simple followers begin to enter into the mystery of love, to be open to the truth that love is possible in our world, that it conquers even death and is for ever. They begin joyfully, excitedly to share this discovery with others.

These first witnesses are driven not by duty, but by love, the love of Jesus in their hearts and the new love they now feel for all others because of him. They are not looking for converts to a new religion. They are sharing incredibly good news. They are sharing a friend who, they believe, is the Son of God. All this they share with those around them who, in turn, believe. These are the people Peter is writing to. They, in turn, share the news with their friends and acquaintances. So the Christian tradition of handing on began, and eventually reached us. Now, as the sharing of this good news spread, there arose opposing voices which rejected this or that part of the message. False teachings and heresies appeared and the early Christian community had to deal with them. Church councils were called to refute the heresies and protect the good news. Dogmas were worked out and creeds formulated to try to put the mystery of Jesus into words. New Christians were then introduced to Jesus through the creeds and the teaching and faith life of a Christian community.

It has to be this way, but we must always be aware of the inevitable danger inherent in this process, that a dogma or creed could take the place of the living person of the Lord. The Christian revelation in Jesus is more than a set of teachings or a creed. The Christian revelation is a person. The good news is Jesus who came not so much to start a new religion as to put us in touch with the living God, and, even more, to share the very life of this God with us. 'I have come so that they may have life and have it to the full' (John 10:10). This very Jesus is risen and among us now, drawing us into the fullness of God. Yes, we meet Jesus in the Creed and believe. But somehow we must meet him in person and know him. He became flesh for this. He was born among us to be close, to win our hearts. The word became flesh. The possible danger of creeds is that the flesh might become words and that a creed might replace the living risen Lord.

Also, when we meet Jesus in the Creed, there is a subtle tendency to stress his divinity. We meet Jesus as true God who is to be adored and obeyed. This can make him seem distant and less real. A further complication is added by our assumption that we know what it means to be divine. For us, divinity means to know all, be all-perfect, have all power, be immune from all suffering. We then impose all these qualities on Jesus and thus push him still further away and widen the gap between him and our 'real' world. Whatever our salvation means, we feel it was accomplished by Jesus exclusively as God. But our faith teaches that Jesus became man to save us. The story of that salvation is in the Gospel.

We have that gospel today. Jesus lives there and speaks his living words to us and reveals himself to us. There we can meet Jesus the man, whom we can come to know as our friend, as one of us, saving us through our humanity which he shares. Then, like our first brothers and sisters in the faith, we are led by Jesus the man to Jesus the Son of God. We do not talk of a 'dead man called Jesus'. We speak of the Lord who is the first risen man, the first of our human kind to pass over into glory. This risen Jesus, still true man, is able to understand our human heart, our struggle, our temptations, our searching. He can listen to our story and speak to our deepest selves so that our hearts too can burn within us as we walk the road of life with him. And this Jesus is true God, not any idol or small god of our fashioning. He is true God, revealing himself as the mystery of love in Jesus, who invites not just the obedience of our intellect, but, also the surrender of our heart. We believe in him, but, much more, we claim we can know him.

Is it not presumptuous for us to speak so confidently about knowing Jesus the Lord, about knowing him who Paul says is 'beyond' all knowledge (Ephesians 3:19). It would be presumptuous if we were claiming we could know the Lord by our own unaided reasoning or desiring. But it is not so. We are given the Holy Spirit precisely to make this possible. We said that the first witnesses knew Jesus as God by faith and that the first generation Christians, who received the good news from those witnesses, also knew and loved Jesus by faith. This was possible only because they had received the Holy Spirit. The same Holy Spirit is given to us today. Jesus tells us what the Spirit will do for us. 'He will teach you everything and remind you of all I have said to you' (John 14:26). And again, 'He will be my witness' (John 15:26). The work of the Holy Spirit is not to take the place of an absent Jesus. It is something more wonderful. His work is to make Jesus present in his new and glorified state. The Holy Spirit comes, not to start a new cult of devotion to himself, but to lead us to Jesus. He witnesses to Jesus and makes Jesus 'real' for us. It is the Holy Spirit who enables you and me today to pass from believing to knowing. With the help of the Holy Spirit, then, let us seek to know and love Jesus, true man and true God.

3

TEMPTED LIKE US

The doctrine of the incarnation, that Jesus Christ is true God and true man, is the very foundation of our Christian faith. Throughout history there have been extremists who have accepted one part of this truth and denied the other. Some have asserted that Jesus is God, and only had the appearance of man. Others have said he was truly a man, the most perfect man, but nothing more. There have been heretics on both sides.

Many Christians may not be as orthodox as they appear. They affirm the doctrine of the incarnation in the creed, but subconsciously stress one side of the truth at the expense of the other. I confess that for many years I was, in this matter, a kind of heretic. I believed firmly in the divinity of Christ, but gave only a notional assent to his humanity. I did not deny the humanity of Jesus, but the humanity I professed was such a watered-down version of human nature that it meant very little to me. It did not nourish my spiritual growth, it did not challenge my faith and did not make Jesus attractive to me as he must have been to his early followers.

I emphasised the biological aspect. Jesus was a man because he was conceived in the womb, grew up like us, ate and slept, was tired and hungry and experienced human emotions. All this is true and wonderful but there is something deeper and more wonderful in the incarnation which I was missing. Emptying himself of divinity to become one of us was not only a biological experience but was also a truly spiritual adventure in which Jesus accepted the full consequences of being human. He laid himself open to fear, danger, darkness, loneliness, helplessness. He was vulnerable not only to the physical violence of his enemies but, worse, to the spiritual violence of temptation. He accepted the ultimate consequence of being human, that he would have to depend totally on another to save him. That other was his Father.

I missed this truth and, for many years, Jesus was for me more like a God dressed up as a man, like an actor on the stage wearing the costume of humanity, acting a part. We know how the great actors can 'live' their parts. They 'become' the character they are portraying for the duration of a play or film. Or, to use another image, Jesus was somewhat like a psychiatrist who, wanting to help his client, studies deeply the complexities of the human psyche so he can enter the inner space of his client and feel with him or her. Von Balthasar gives another image of such impoverished notions of the incarnation, the image of a teacher: 'Jesus came to show us how to live, like a teacher writing on the blackboard the solution of a problem which presents no difficulty to him, since he has no part in the laborious efforts of his pupils.' All these false understandings of the incarnation have one thing in common – that Jesus did not endure the full consequences of being human, that it really did not cost him, that the divinity was always there to protect and save him. I do not know how I missed the clear message in Paul's words: Jesus 'did not cling to his equality with God but emptied himself to assume the condition of a slave and became as men are; and being as all men are, he was humbler yet, even to accepting death, death on a cross' (Philippians 2:6-8).

The Letter to the Hebrews says Jesus was able to feel our weaknesses with us because he 'has been tempted in every way that we are, though he is without sin' (Hebrews 4:15). This inspired word, which stressed the genuine humanity of Jesus had a curious stumbling-block in it for me. I had the strange idea that this sinlessness made Jesus less human, that he would be closer to me if he had experienced sin. Time was needed for me to realise that the more truly human a person is, the more he or she will live from love, the more sinless that person will be. The truly human person is the one who is moved to compassion, who goes out to others, who puts love and not self at the centre. Jesus was tempted to sin. He was pulled towards evil away from love, but he held on to love even to the point of death. So he can understand us when we are pulled by evil and even when we surrender to the evil. He can hold out a hand to pull us back. He can save.

This is what makes Jesus so attractive. I should have realised this when I read in the gospel that the sinners flocked to him (Luke 15:1). Sin turns one back to self, away from God and others. Sin separates. Sinlessness, which is unselfish love, draws Jesus closer to me. Sinners flocked to Jesus because he was a perfect man who had also experienced temptation but who overcame it with love and trust. It was because he was truly human, truly one of us, and despite suffering and temptation, could still believe in the Father's love, it was because of all this that he could touch hidden springs in people's hearts. There was no judgment in him. True love never makes the other feel small or mean or inferior. Jesus echoed the deepest good self in others.

The inspired word of scripture says Jesus was tempted like us. What can it mean to say Jesus was tempted? Very often, when Christians speak of sin, they think of sexual sins and when they think of temptation, they think of temptation to such sins. This very limited and childish understanding of sin obscures the terrible variety of evil which abounds in our world and buffets the heart, evil that surfaces within us or attacks from without. We must not trivialise the very painful reality of temptation by reducing it to sexual temptation. When Jesus was asked what was the most important commandment, he said that it was love, and he summarised all law under the twofold command, to love God and our neighbour. The great temptation then is to act against love, to put self at the centre and act out of selfish motives, to pull away from others and refuse love. Jesus was one of us, a truly human person. He had an immense love and compassion for all people. This love for others, which was nourished by his love for God his Father, was the meaning of his life. But being truly like us this love did not come easily to him. It did not just happen. It involved heroic unselfishness and temptation which on one occasion produced a sweat of blood from his body (Luke 22:44).

The classic scripture passage about the temptation of Jesus is the temptation in the desert after the baptism in the Jordan. Remember that the short gospel account is a summary of days and weeks of struggle. It was not simply a matter of Jesus' hearing a voice inviting him to work a miracle and then replying to it with a text of scripture and that was the end of it. No! It was real temptation, real interior struggle going on for days. The tempting voice did not come only from outside Jesus. It was echoing within him. Jesus was feeling this could be all right. I am hungry. I need food. Why not work a miracle! But his truer self resisted and saw that this would be going back on his agreement to be fully human, to being truly dependent on power outside himself, truly relying on his Father. He has emptied himself of divinity out of love for us. He will accept the full consequences of his choice. There is interior struggle and pain, but he wins through. He resists the temptation. He does not sin.

Notice how the temptation is introduced, 'If you are the Son' (Matthew 4:3). Here is an attack on his identity, an attack on his trust in the Father. The essential temptation is always the same, to sow distrust in God's word, in God's love. So it was in the beginning in the garden. The serpent tried to sow doubt. 'Did God really say you were not to eat from any of the trees in the garden?' (Genesis 3:1). The first man and woman listened and were deceived. Now there is a similar scenario in the desert. The temptation is subtle. 'If you are the Son. Perhaps you are not the Son! If God were truly your Father, how could he allow you to be hungry? After all, what father would give his son a stone when he needs bread?' The devil tries to sow doubt in this man. But this is a new Adam, a new man and he will not listen to the tempter's word, but only to his Father's word. That will be his food, his nourishment for life's struggle. He will show all of us that all who trust like that will not be ashamed.

The devil takes Jesus to the temple top and invites him to cast himself down. Again it is temptation; test your so-called Father. Scripture says he will not let you suffer. Cast yourself down, work a great miracle, people will be in awe and will worship. It will be a quick, easy, painless way of winning people to your side. What a plausible temptation, one which finds an echo in our hearts. But to agree would be to deny the incarnation, it would be clinging to divinity and evading the full consequences of being human. It would be failure to trust his Father and would avoid identifying with suffering people. There is another way, the way of being fully human, whatever it may bring, the way his Father wants and which he has accepted. Jesus did not argue this out calmly and easily. He was tired, weary, hungry. He battled with the tension within him; the pull of his human nature towards an easy and glorious way and the deeper wisdom of the Father which would lead eventually to Calvary.

The battle is not over when Jesus emerges from the desert. At a later time he will suffer the full consequences of this choice to be human, to be like us in all things. The temptation will recur and he will be reduced to a sweat of blood. St Luke finishes the account of the desert temptation with ominous words: 'The devil left him, to return at the appointed time' (Luke 4:13). Gethsemane is the appointed place and Holy Thursday the time. Jesus again faces his tempter who will make a last desperate play to turn this man away from the path of love. 'This is your hour; this is the reign of darkness' (Luke 22:53). In the garden he feels the full weight of his very real humanity. 'And a sudden fear came over him, and great distress. And he said to them, "My soul is sorrowful to the point of death" ' (Mark 14:33-34). He is so lonely and afraid. The forces of organised religion, of self-righteous, holy people, of ambitious politicians, are all combined against him and he is brought so low he wants to call it all off. 'Father! Everything is possible for you. Take this cup away from me' (Mark 14:36).

But once again, as in the desert, he holds on and trusts his Father. 'But let it be as you, not I, would have it' (Mark 14:36). He is not abandoned. He receives just enough power to cope, to hang on, to remain faithful to love, to the Father, to you and me. For let us take note that all this is for us. Through it all he is saying, 'It is possible to hold on, to trust, to love.' This is what the incarnation means. This is how he is saving us. We look at this man, our brother, and ask the help of the Holy Spirit that we may understand what we see. Then, when we try to be like him, to love and trust like him, we are starting to experience the salvation he brought.

4

FAMILIAR WITH SUFFERING

We are exploring some of the deeper implications of the incarnation in the hope that this will lead us to a new appreciation of the wonder of Jesus' love for us. Surely we must be drawn in a new way to our Saviour when we realise how he accepted our human nature in all its frailty and limitations, how he was truly tempted to give in to fear and selfishness, how he emptied himself of divinity to walk the lonely road of a limited human person and how he did all this for us. Will our hearts not be moved when we realise how like us he was and yet how he kept on reaching out to people despite disappointment, failure, misunderstanding, even rejection? Will we not want, as fellow human beings, to congratulate our Lord, to admire and thank him and believe more sincerely what he is telling us, that love is possible in our world? He invites us to follow him in this way, with total trust in our heavenly Father, and to be truly human in the best sense, thus bringing more light and beauty into our world.

We considered briefly two high points of temptation in the life of Jesus, the desert and the garden. We can be sure that the deeper currents of our frail human nature which surfaced on those occasions were flowing all the time and that Jesus, like all of us, had his dark and low moments when he wanted to give it all up, to run away from it all and question why he should be his brother's keeper. There must have been times when he was tempted to anger with his enemies. Did he not feel a struggle within when James and John wanted to call down fire on those towns which rejected him? These are the thoughts of men and Jesus is a man. When Peter protested at Caesarea Philippi that Jesus would not have to endure suffering, the desert temptation must have flared up again. His sharp rebuke to Peter reveals deep inner emotion, upset and struggle. Peter is speaking the thoughts not of God but of humankind. 'The way you think is not God's way but man's' (Mark 8:33). Jesus will think only the thoughts of God, but as a man he feels the pull of our thoughts. We have an expression of great frustrated disappointment with his dull and uncomprehending disciples when he says to them, 'Do you not yet understand? Have you no perception? Are your minds closed? Have you eyes that do not see, ears that do not hear?' (Mark 8:17-18). And what a great weariness must have swept over him to move him to tears over Jerusalem.

The greatest temptation and the greatest victory and the supreme revelation of God's love was, of course, Calvary. Here is the final emptying, not only of divinity but of his very humanity. Here again the desert temptation is echoed. The crowd is shouting, 'If you are God's Son, come down from the cross!' (Matthew 27:40). In the desert the tempter had said, 'If you are the Son of God, throw yourself down' (Matthew 4:6), in that way you will win the admiration and support of the crowd. Here now it is the very crowd itself calling on him to work the miracle and come down from the cross. In the desert, the tempter assured him that he would not suffer: 'Angels will support you on their hands in case you hurt your foot against a stone' (Matthew 4:6). Notice that in Satan's picture of God there is no place for suffering. But this is not God's wisdom. For God the only absolute is love, and to be true to love will involve suffering.

Jesus is the love of God made visible. What keeps him on the cross is not nails or ropes but love. He cannot come down. He would contradict himself if he did. If he came down he would not be God for God is love. But let us try to be sensitive to the struggle going on in his humanity as he hangs there. We are so familiar with the Calvary scene. We can be tempted to glamorise it and inoculate ourselves against the dark mystery of this young man hanging there, sacrificing himself in total unselfish love for so many who do not care and entering into that deepest, darkest place for him, the sense of being abandoned by his beloved Abba as he cries out, 'My God, my God, why have you deserted me?' (Mark 15:34). Yes, he is grievously tempted but will hold on blindly to his trust in this Father.

As we stand and watch Jesus let us believe that the Father stands beside us. This is not mere fantasy. We are witnessing the mystery hidden from all time, the mystery of the ultimate expression of the love of the Most Blessed Trinity for you and me. We are loved and saved by Father, Son and Holy Spirit. St Paul says 'Love endures everything'. Jesus now endures all, only because of this total trust in the Father's love for himself and for us, a love which is poured out on him and us by the Holy Spirit. All this is for us as we stand and contemplate. We stand beside the Father. We look at the Son, our brother. And the Spirit is upon us to understand what we contemplate.

One of our temptations as we stand there could be to experience fear or guilt. But neither of these is a Spirit response. The Spirit, which is given us as the fruit of what we contemplate, casts out fear, heals guilt and pours out love. We are involved in the greatest act of love. We are not witnessing an act of punishment. But maybe we should qualify that statement. Is Jesus being punished on Calvary? Yes, he is being punished, but certainly not by his beloved Father. He is being punished by people for being different, for answering evil with love, for challenging self-righteousness and pride, for identifying with the poor and sinners, for challenging power structures which would debase and destroy the image of God in people.

But certainly he is not being punished by his heavenly Father who stands beside us. Jesus is the Beloved Son in whom the Father is well pleased. Think of that gentle Father whom Jesus described in the story of the Prodigal Son. That's how Jesus understood his Father and he claimed that no one understood the Father except the Son (Matthew 11:27). In that story Jesus told us how the father of the prodigal missed his boy and watched every day for his return, how he saw the boy when he was far off and was moved to pity, how he ran down the road to meet him and welcome him. We stand by the Father now and look at this other Son on the cross. He too left his Father's house for a distant place. He too took with him his Father's riches to scatter them in a prodigal way among us, his sinner friends. But now he is tired and weary and broken and would like to arise and go back to his dear Father. Do you not think that this Father saw his boy Jesus when he was far off on that hill of Calvary, that he was moved to a great pity and that he has run here to embrace him?

The father of the prodigal embraced his son in all his rags, covered with the dirt of the journey. This Son on the cross is badly disfigured from his journey amongst us. The prophet says:

> Without beauty, without majesty,
> no looks to attract our eyes;
> a thing despised and rejected by men,
> a man of sorrows and familiar with suffering,
> a man to make people screen their faces.
> *Isaiah 53:2-3*

I don't think the Father on Calvary screened his face because he does not judge by appearances. It is only we who do that. 'God does not see as man sees; man looks at appearances but Yahweh looks at the heart' (1 Samuel 16:7). The father of the prodigal saw the repentant heart of his boy under the rags of his sins and he embraced the boy on the road. On Calvary, the Father sees the great loving heart of his Son under all the disfigurement of his passion and lovingly takes the boy into his embrace when he says, 'Father, into your hands I commit my Spirit.' This embrace is the resurrection. We can imagine this Father joyfully announcing to all, 'We are going to have a feast, a celebration, because this Son of mine was dead and has come back to life' (Luke 15:24).

What will we say to this Father? How can we thank him? We can borrow God's very own words to praise him, the words Yahweh spoke to Abraham when that father was prepared to sacrifice his only son Isaac out of loving trust in Yahweh. These words can now be our prayer. God said to Abraham, 'Because you have not refused me your son, your only son, I will shower blessings on you' (Genesis 22:17). God has not refused us his Son, his only Son. Will we not forever, in the power of the Spirit, shower blessings and praise on God our Father and Jesus his Son, our brother?

Satan had it so wrong in the desert. The crowd had it so wrong on Calvary. You and I have it so wrong today. Our wisdom is so puny and shortsighted. 'Avoid pain at all cost, even at the cost of betraying love.' In the desert Satan invited Jesus to cast himself down from the temple top, assuring him that angels would lift him up lest he hurt his foot. But God had another way. Not angels but people would lift up his Son and lift him up in pain. But by this very lifting up on the cross, he will draw all people to himself. The seed will die on Calvary and produce an everlasting harvest.

5

LET GO THE BRANCH

When St Paul invites us to become other Christs, when he says to us, 'In your minds you must be the same as Christ Jesus' (Philippians 2:5), it seems as if he is proposing an impossible ideal. The gap between the sinless Christ and myself seems unbridgeable. But when we take the incarnation more seriously, when we look upon Christ in his humanity and in his full acceptance of all the limitations that implied, we can begin to have a better idea of what Paul is proposing. Jesus emptied himself and lived a life of total trust in his Father's loving providence. He worked no miracles for himself but depended completely on his Father. Jesus lived this life of trust out to the very end when his Father seemed far away, as on Calvary. Shortly after crying out, 'My God, my God, why have you forsaken me?', he can serenely let go his life and fall back into his Father's arms. It is here in this life of total trust in the Father that you and I can be like our Saviour.

Consider this modern humorous parable. An atheist who is a keen mountain climber is climbing a high and difficult peak. He is all alone, way up on the mountain height. He is crawling along a narrow ridge. He moves with great care as there is an immense drop over the side. Then, despite all his experience, his foot slips and he tumbles over the edge. A small tree is growing out of the wall of the cliff and as he falls he grabs a branch of the tree. Hanging there and peering down into the depths below, he has second thoughts about religion and cries out to God for help. The only answer to his cry is the echo of his own voice. He tries again, 'Oh, God, help me and I will believe in you!' Again the only answer is an echo. He cries out again, 'Please, God, help me. If you help me I will do anything you ask.' This time the silence is broken by a mighty voice booming out over the valley. The voice says, 'That's

what they all say when they are in trouble.' The excited converted atheist shouts back, 'No, God. I am different from the
others. I really will do anything you ask.' 'All right then',
answers the voice, 'let go the branch!'

This little parable describes the bottom line of faith. 'Let go
the branch.' I have a poster which shows a kitten hanging
from a height and looking down in terror. The caption reads,
'Faith is not faith, till it's all you have to hang on to.'

'Let go the branch.' To me this is what Jesus had to do on
Calvary. He hung from the tree of the cross very much alone.
Friends had deserted him. The leaders had rejected him and
even God seemed far away. His act of death was a letting-go
of the branch of the tree of the cross. It was his own deliber-
ate act of trust. 'No one takes my life from me; I lay it down
of my own free will' (John 10:18). He let go and fell back into
his Father's arms. He is safely caught and lifted back to life.
It is because of this immense trust that we, his followers, can
serenely let go in death and know that we do not plunge
into any abyss but fall gently into the Father's arms.

In a beautiful scripture image God said that he carried his
chosen people to safety 'on eagle's wings' (Exodus19:4). I
never realised the beauty and power of this image until a
scripture scholar explained it to me. The mighty eagle lives
way up in the high mountain peaks. It nests on a narrow
ledge overlooking the deep valley. There the eagle hatches
her young. When it is time to train the young birds to fly, the
mother takes a young bird and places it on her back and
then flies out over the valley. At a great height the mother
bird turns over and drops the bird into space. The little bird
tumbles helplessly down through the air. As it falls, it furi-
ously flaps its stunted wings. As yet they are not sufficiently
developed to enable the young bird to fly successfully. All
the while, the mother eagle is circling round the little bird as
it plummets down. After some minutes, the mother bird
sweeps under the fledgling, catches it on her broad wing
and gently flies back up to the ledge and safety.

In his teaching, Jesus invited us to look at the birds of the air and learn from them about our heavenly Father and his concern for us. If a mother eagle can so care for her young and not allow it to fall to destruction, what about our heavenly Father? Will he allow his beloved Son Jesus to fall to destruction and final death? Jesus banked his life on the certainty that his Father would catch him. His trust was vindicated. Our faith says he did all this for us. He lived for us, he died for us and he rose for us. What are we learning as we contemplate his death and resurrection? Are we discovering the hidden meaning and being nourished?

The seed dies on Calvary, only to bear much fruit in us. Having died it will not remain alone (John 12:24). We today can experience the power of this great trust and love. We can experience it not only in the great final act of death, but in the many other death-like situations which recur in life when all seems dark and hopeless and God seems far away. To put all our trust in God then will seem like letting go the branch. We may have to make a decision or choose a course of action which seems to promise something like death. We may have to give up a relationship without which we feel we could not live. We may have to kick a habit without which life would not seem worth living. Jesus assures us that it is possible to let go and that his Father who is our Father will be faithful. We will not plunge into the abyss we dread. It is not all dark below. There may be some cloud obscuring the view, but the ultimate sustaining reality is love.

Calvary is a drama. Good drama reflects and interprets life. In this drama of Calvary we are not mere spectators. We are involved. The young man hanging on the cross is one of the family and he is doing this for us. He is showing us that it is possible to endure the worst that can happen and eventually to let go in total trust. The drama of Calvary, like any good play, surrenders its meaning only slowly. No great drama or play will be fully appreciated on a first reading or performance. Deeper meaning is revealed as years pass by and I come to the play with more personal experience of life's joys and sorrows. Surely I will see and grasp more of life in Hamlet now than when I first met it in my schooldays. So, over the years, the drama of Calvary invites me into a deeper appreciation of the mystery of God's love for me.

In a sense, the very fact that in our faith we wish to come to Calvary in prayer and stand before a cross speaks of mystery. Let us not glamorise the cross. Remember it was an instrument of degrading torture. It was a shameful punishment and death reserved for slave and criminal. Scripture says, 'Cursed be everyone who is hanged on a tree' (Galatians 3:13). After the death of Jesus we could have expected that his first followers would want to forget about this part of the story, to rewrite this chapter of his history, to hide all references to the cross. But the opposite happens. The crucified Saviour is at the heart of their preaching. The crucified Lord who rose is the Good News. And the cross on which he hung is celebrated in creed, liturgy, song, art and literature. Crosses are fashioned in wood, stone and precious metal. They are raised high on buildings, they adorn altars and graves. They are carried in pockets, worn about the neck. Why? because the human heart reads the Calvary scene correctly and understands that the theme of this drama is love and that we are the object of that love, and so Paul understands the cross as 'God's power to save' (1 Corinthians 1:18).

In April 1986, in the Ukrainian town of Chernobyl, there was an explosion in a nuclear plant. The explosion threw up an invisible radioactive dust which contaminated and poisoned the surrounding district. Over 130,000 people were evacuated from their homes. A wasteland was left behind. The poisonous dust spewed out by the explosion was carried to lands far beyond the border. Its destructive effects were felt thousands of miles away from Chernobyl and for years after the explosion. We have been reflecting on Calvary. Can we not say that two thousand years ago on the hill of Calvary there was an explosion of love which sent great waves of power out over the whole world? This power does not maim or destroy or poison, it heals and restores and beautifies all it touches. It falls on the waste-land of human hearts and under its gentle touch that wasteland rejoices and blossoms into new and beautiful life. This power we speak of which now heals and re-creates is the power which originally created all being. It is the power of love and it has no borders of place or time. And all this is so, because of Calvary, because there was a man, one of ourselves, who had enough trust to let go the branch.

6

THE HIDDEN THINGS OF GOD

We have been contemplating Jesus, a man like us in all things. He is not a God dressed up and and playing a part. He is truly one of us from the womb to the tomb. He accepts the full consequences of being human, even, as Paul says, to the point of death. He walks through our world as the embodiment of love. He is the man who lives for others. He reaches out in love and compassion to all people. This, he tells us, is what it means to be truly human. He is able to live like this because he is certain that the ultimate reality is love. He is the man of supreme trust. His name for God is Abba, a loving, caring Father. He can walk in love because he walks in trust. The source of his love for people is this God, who, he believes, is love itself. The source of his power to heal people, both their bodies and spirits, is the Father's love. He walks in unwavering trust in that reality of God's love even into the valley of death and beyond.

Let us enter more deeply into the Mystery of Jesus. This same Jesus who is perfect man is also revealing the inner being of God. He can say, 'No one knows the Father except the Son and those to whom the Son chooses to reveal him' (Matthew 11:27). One day Philip, one of the Twelve, asked Jesus to show them the Father. Jesus answered, 'To have seen me is to have seen the Father' (John 14:9). If we want to know what God is like, we must look at Jesus. We said earlier in this book that many Christians first meet Jesus in the Creed as true God to be adored. And we noted an inherent difficulty there, namely that we assume that we know what divinity means and we impose these assumptions on Jesus. But Jesus says that no one knows God except his Son. Should we not let Jesus teach us what it means to be divine? Fr Nolan OP puts it well when he writes, 'Divinity has nothing to teach us about Jesus, but Jesus has much to teach us about divinity.'

The first followers met Jesus, the man, who led them on to discover God. In the Letter to the Hebrews, Jesus is described thus: 'He is the radiant light of God's glory and the perfect copy of his nature' (Hebrews 1:3). St Paul says, 'He is the image of the unseen God' (Colossians 1:15). Today we would say that Jesus is the image of his Father. Parents are pleased and complimented when friends notice and point out resemblances between child and parents. They are happy when someone says about the new baby, 'She has her mother's eyes' or 'She has her father's smile'. They are more pleased if, later on, deeper resemblances are noted; when someone says, 'He has his father's love for the truth' or 'He has his mother's compassion for the sick'. Jesus is the perfect image of his heavenly Father. He reflects the Father to us and thus teaches us what divinity means.

When we say Jesus teaches us about divinity, we are not saying that it is an easy lesson to learn. The first followers were very slow learners, just as we are today. We say Jesus the man led them to know God, but, as we have noted, the road to that discovery led past a hill called Calvary. That's where the difficulty lay for them, as for us and all believers. God's revelation of himself in Jesus does not fit our preconceived ideas of God. St Paul describes the qualities we all expect to find in God. 'The Jews demand miracles and the Greeks look for wisdom' (1 Corinthians 1:22). In popular thinking God is power and miracle. This is the language of philosophy. Paul says the God revealed by Jesus cannot be preached in this language. Paul speaks of the 'foolishness' and the 'weakness' of God and asks, 'Where are the philosophers now?' (1 Corinthians 1:20). Surely these words from Paul must be inspired. Otherwise he would have to be accused of blasphemy. No Jew could have dared to apply such words as 'foolish' or 'weak' to Yahweh.

We say the road to the discovery of God in Jesus lay past the hill of Calvary. Up to that point his followers had very unclear ideas about their master. But one thing would have been certain in their thinking, that suffering should not be part of the story. However, this is the lonely and unpopular road Jesus takes and it was only after the trauma of crucifixion, followed by resurrection and the gift of the Holy Spirit, that his followers enter into God's wisdom and confess that Jesus was truly God's Son, the perfect image of his Father.

If we today are slow to recognise God behind the mask of suffering, we can take heart when we remember how slow St Peter was and how patient Jesus was with him. One day, when Jesus foretold his suffering and death, Peter protested strongly. 'Taking him aside, Peter started to remonstrate with him. "Heaven preserve you Lord, this must not happen to you" ' (Matthew 16:22). Peter speaks for all of us here. It is good that Jesus should be the Messiah, but unacceptable that the Messiah should suffer. We all want a Messiah, a God of glory, success, miracles. We do not want a Messiah who suffers. Notice the strong word Jesus uses when he corrects Peter: 'Get behind me Satan! You are an obstacle in my path, because the way you think is not God's way but man's' (Matthew 16:23). Jesus calls Peter Satan because he echoes the desert temptation when Satan tried to persuade Jesus to take an easy road to glory and avoid all suffering.

Satan's idea of God is our idea. God can only mean glory, power, success, miracles. Satan, Peter and all of us have to learn that God means love. Peter echoes Satan's idea and our hearts'. Jesus says to us all, 'The way you think is not God's way but man's.' Jesus has come to show us God's way, as far above our way as the heavens are above the earth. God's wisdom appears like foolishness to us. But it is God's wisdom and it is love. In some way Satan must have sensed this. Notice what Satan fears in Jesus. He does not fear power or strength or miracles. Indeed he encourages all this. But he deeply fears the weakness of Jesus shown in his suffering, for in there is hiding the only kind of power Satan fears, the power of love. Jesus is revealing God's wisdom and power. This is what it means to be God, to go the whole way in love, to empty oneself in love. This is not only perfect humanity, but is also what it means to be divine. And we are created in the image and likeness of this God. We are invited to be like our God, to love as Jesus loved, to empty ourselves for each other, even to lose our lives for each other. Something deep inside us tells us this is not impossible. When we try to love, the divine spark within us is kindled. To be his disciples in this way, to learn this lesson, involves long, slow, hard study in the school of life. Much of the homework involves suffering! This suffering can be a stumbling-block, but it can also be the doorway into that mysterious place where we touch divinity in Jesus and in our own selves.

In the desert Satan said that God would not let his Son suffer and he further suggested that if suffering did come, then he was not the beloved Son. Those who mocked Christ on Calvary used the same kind of reasoning. 'He put his trust in God; now let God rescue him if he wants him. For he did say, 'I am the Son of God' (Matthew 27:44). It is the same suggestion. 'If he is God's Son as he claims, then this should not be happening to him.' The conclusion of the crowd on Calvary, whose thoughts were human thoughts, was, 'God is not his Father.' The true conclusion should have been, 'We do not understand God and his mysterious ways.'

In the Book of Wisdom we have another example of human thinking, failing completely to comprehend the wisdom of God. There we read how wicked men plot against God's holy prophet. They plan to condemn the prophet to a shameful death. They say to each other, 'Let us see if what he says is true' (Wisdom 2:17). What had the prophet said? 'He calls himself a Son of the Lord, and boasts of having God for his father' (Wisdom 2:13,16). We see their argument: God could not let his beloved messenger suffer. So, if he does suffer, then it means God is not really his father. Here is the same human wisdom which cannot fathom the depths of God's ways. These men think like Satan, like Peter, like the crowd on Calvary, like me and you. The Book of Wisdom comments thus:

> This is the way they reason, but they are misled,
> their malice makes them blind.
> They do not know the hidden things of God.
> *Wisdom 2: 21-22*

Let us ask Jesus to touch our eyes, to remove our blindness and to teach us the hidden things of God. Let us ask him to help us to know our heavenly Father so that we can better understand and follow his word to us: 'You must therefore be perfect just as your heavenly Father is perfect' (Matthew 5:48).

7

'PRESENTE'

In the early hours of 16 November 1989, armed men entered the residence of the Jesuit-run Central American University in San Salvador and murdered six Jesuit priests and two women domestics, a mother and her sixteen-year-old daughter. At a requiem mass for these martyrs held in Lusaka in Zambia, a Jesuit priest preached the homily. He spoke with great feeling because he had lived in El Salvador and knew personally those who had been murdered. In the homily he reminded us that members of the basic Christian communities in Central and South America are no strangers to torture and death. He told us that when these communities meet for the Eucharist, they pray for those members of the community who have been slain. They have a roll-call for their members. The name of the murdered person is still called out and the congregation answers 'Presente'. This beautiful response of faith asserts that death is not final, that loved ones still live, that our union with them is not destroyed by death. In some real mysterious way in spirit and in truth they are 'presente'.

This kind of faith is possible because Jesus had enough trust to let go of his young life and let himself fall back into his Father's arms. 'Father, into your hands I commit my Spirit' (Luke 23:46). If these South American Christians can call out 'Presente' for their martyred dead, it is only because we, with equal faith, hope and love, can shout out 'Presente' for our crucified saviour, Jesus Christ. And this is what we do at every Eucharist at the proclamation of faith when we all say, 'Christ is risen, Christ will come again.' In another form of the proclamation we say, 'Dying you destroyed our death, rising you restored our life. Lord Jesus come in glory.'

The mystery of God's love affair with us is not exhausted by his death for us on the cross. St Paul says, 'He not only died for us – he rose from the dead, and there at God's right hand he stands and pleads for us' (Romans 8:34). Jesus rose from the dead for us. We might be inclined to think he died for us but that he rose for himself! The mystery is deeper. He rose to tell us that those who put their trust in God will not be abandoned. His rising tells us that love can overcome hate, that love is possible and is the ultimate reality. He rose to tell us that we will rise. He rose to take our humanity into glory. He did not discard his humanity after Calvary as a worker might hang up her overalls after completing a job. And he rose to be with us all the days of our pilgrimage through life. We can at any moment say his name and hear him whisper to our hearts, 'Presente', I am with you.

At the Easter vigil liturgy all over the world, groups of people, large and small, gather under the night sky around the Paschal fire. It is a very symbolic act, a community gathered round a fire at night. The fire, especially when out in the open night air, offers light, warmth, protection. The fire attracts and gathers a community round itself. And what do people do when gathered round a fire? Often they tell stories. They tell stories of the family, of the nation. A story may be told about some member of the family who was wise in leadership; one who did great things and brought pride and glory to the family.

At Easter the Christian family gathers round the Paschal fire and tells again the story of the great deed done by the eldest Son, the first-born of the family, Jesus Christ. It is the story of how he challenged the evil powers of darkness, even death itself, on behalf of the whole family and won a great victory. It was a terrible battle and it cost him his young life, but it was done out of love and, in dying for love, he proved what our hearts always secretly believed, that love is for ever. We can never tire of this story and, each year, as children do, we turn to our Mother, the Church and say, 'Tell it again.'

This elder brother, our dear Lord and Saviour, is risen

and present among us, offering us a share in the victory he has won over evil, fear, sin and selfishness.

> Yahweh your God is in your midst,
> a victorious warrior.
> He will exult with joy over you,
> he will renew you by his love.
> *Zephaniah 3:17*

The victory was for us. We are chosen in him from the beginning by the Father. 'Before the world was made, he chose us, chose us in Christ, to live through love in his presence' (Ephesians 1:4). Without him we can do nothing. But we are not without him. He is with us in intimate union. 'I am the vine, you are the branches' (John 15:5). It is interesting to notice that in the Old Testament the image of the vine was used, but in that instance we were the vine. Yahweh plants a choice vine hoping for good grapes, but his people fail to produce good fruit. 'He expected it to yield grapes, but sour grapes were all that it gave' (Isaiah 5:2). But now, in our day, Jesus is the vine and we are the branches. We can be fruitful because we draw life from him who is risen and with us.

Let us go deeper. The resurrection of Jesus our brother is part of the mystery of God's plan for us, hidden from all eternity but now revealed in our time in Jesus. The resurrection is not a matter of turning the tables on Satan or evil. It is not merely the reversing of a bad situation. We are witnessing planned fulfilment. It is not a question of Jesus being brought back to this life and taking up where he had left off, thus frustrating all his enemies. We are witnessing the flowering of the seed that died in trust. Jesus does not come back to our limited form of life. He moves forward into the new life of glory. It is a passover. And where he has gone, each of us can follow. This is our destiny. Death is not something that falls upon us or something which catches us out or cuts short a life. It is our passover into glory.

And more still. The fruit of the resurrection of our Saviour is for us now. It is not only a consolation that awaits us after death. It is new life offered us right now, today. Our passover can begin now. We can rise today out of the many death experiences that rob us of light, warmth, joy and peace. Such experiences are fear, loneliness, guilt, anger, addiction and doubt. We are invited by him who is the victorious warrior, who is risen and present, to experience even today a passover from such enemies. So it was for his first followers. The death of their friend Jesus left them in a world of shattered dreams, a world of darkness, confusion and hopelessness. Then they too experienced him among them saying 'Presente'. They rose into a new experience of joy, hope and love that was so strong that they could face even the enemy, death, smiling.

That experience of Jesus as Risen Lord present to his followers and sharing with them his victory over fear and death was, above all, a love experience. The Jesus who suffered, died and rose for them is present among them because he cares, because he loves them. They feel precious and lovable in his eyes, and he is God. The experience of being loved in this way, despite their weakness, is the source of extraordinary new courage, power and joy. This love, and the power it brings, will sustain them in all of life's trials and sorrows. Ultimately, only love can give the power to endure everything. Jesus is that love in the lives of those early followers. We are told that when Peter and the apostles were flogged for speaking to the people about Jesus, they considered it a great honour to suffer for the Lord (Acts 5:41). St Paul had his life turned upside down on the Damascus road when he was convinced that Jesus was alive and not dead and, much more, that Jesus knew his name, loved him and had died for him. From now on this love is the great reality in Paul's life. The values that had previously motivated him are as nothing compared to Christ's love. 'I look on everything as so much rubbish if only I can have Christ' (Philippians 3:8).

As it was for those first friends, so it must be for all Christ's followers of any and every age. For each of us Jesus died, is risen and is with us in love. That love must be the source of all our power to bear life's sorrows. It must also be the love story that brings sunshine, warmth and joy into our lives. Over the years, it is to be hoped that this love will grow and become our treasure. The growth may be slow and gradual because we are weak. That's all right. Paul accepts this for himself and for us when he says that we carry this treasure which is Christ 'in earthenware jars' (2 Corinthians 4:7). But gradually we begin to realise that Christ's steadfast love is real treasure beside which the world's wealth and pleasures lose much of their attraction. Here is a story.

> One evening a pilgrim, known for holiness, arrived at the outskirts of an Indian village. He spread his prayer mat and had begun to pray when a man from the village came through the bush, approached him and said: 'Holy man, I have had a dream about you and in the dream was told to ask you for a very special stone you carry.' The pilgrim at first seemed puzzled but then his face brightened and he began to rummage in the leather bag which carried all his possessions. As he was doing so, he said he had found an unusual stone on the forest path. He then took out from the bag a large shinning diamond. Holding it up, he said, 'It is indeed unusual and beautiful, Do you want it?' The villager tried to conceal his desire and joy. 'Yes! Yes, that's the stone. May I have it?' The pilgrim handed him the diamond. The villager grabbed it and rushed off, fearing the pilgrim might change his mind, but the holy man was already absorbed in prayer. Next morning, as the pilgrim was at morning prayer, he was again distracted by

45

someone coming through the bush. He looked up and saw the same villager standing there with the diamond in his hand. This time, the villager went down on his knees beside the pilgrim and said he wished to return the diamond. 'Oh', said the pilgrim, 'do you not like it?' The villager answered 'It is beautiful and very valuable, but I wish to return it. You see, all night, I have not slept wondering what treasure you must possess that enables you to give away a most precious diamond with such ease and peace. I now beg you humbly to share this other treasure with me.'

For the Christian believer, the other treasure is surely the personal love of Jesus for each of us. That love is unconditional. It is offered to us because we are his, because we belong to him and he sees us as lovable. We say his love is unconditional, but, in fact, there is one condition we must fulfil before we can experience this love. That condition may seem easy, but for many it seems to prove difficult. The condition is that we accept the love that is offered. Why is it that we are so slow to accept this love in a child-like way? One reason, I believe, is that we feel that we are not worthy of it. If only we could realise that the whole point about unconditional love is that we do not have to be worthy. Indeed, it is a contradiction to speak of being worthy of unconditional love. Its like asking about the price of a free gift! A gift is given because we are loved, not because we pay a price.

8

COME WITHOUT MONEY

We live in *anno domini*, the time of Christ our Lord. This year is his year. Our destiny, earthly and eternal, is bound up with him. We are chosen in him before time began. He is among us, offering us a teaching which gives meaning to our lives, but he offers much more. He offers his life. He invites us into a personal love relationship with him. This love is the source of the new life and power that can be ours. One of the great stumbling-blocks to our experiencing this loving, empowering presence, to our growing in a deepening love relationship with Jesus, is our sense of unworthiness. We feel we are not worthy of this love. How could people so small and insignificant as us be noticed and desired by the Lord? How could people so sinful and unfaithful as us be offered this relationship of love and power?

First of all, let us be aware that all we have been speaking about is known to us only by revelation. It is not a human programme, it is not a religious ideology proposed by Church leaders. It is not the end-product of the reasoning of some noble human philosopher. We are speaking of good news revealed to us by the transcendent God. We speak of a message, an invitation from God's own heart, a message spoken many times through holy messengers and prophets and now, in our day, through his beloved Son (Hebrews1:1-2).

Ask yourself whom Jesus was addressing when he spoke the good news and revealed the secrets of his Father's heart. He was talking to the most ordinary simple people, country folk, village and town dwellers. Most were illiterate and without formal education. Many were poor, oppressed and marginalised. They were acquainted with human weakness and failure. They were familiar with fear, anger, hatred, poverty, prostitution, guilt and corruption.

This is the human condition, then, now, always. And Jesus knew all this. We can see from the great variety of characters in his many stories how well he understood the complexity of the human heart. It is to these very people that he comes with his message of new life and his offer of love.

And he rejoices to have this mission. 'It was then that, filled with joy by the Holy Spirit, he said, "I bless you, Father, Lord of heaven and earth, for hiding these things from the learned and the clever and revealing them to mere children"' (Luke 10:21). To such people he offers a new intimacy with God. If anyone accepts him and tries to follow the way he shows them, 'my Father will love him, and we shall come to him and make our home with him' (John 14:23). What news for people who made annual pilgrimage to Jerusalem and considered it a privilege and a glory to be able to enter the great temple, the very house of Yahweh!

> How I rejoiced when they said to me,
> 'Let us go to the house of Yahweh!'
> And now our feet are standing
> in your gateways, Jerusalem.
> *Psalm 122:1-2*

And now they are told that they themselves can be the very house of God and that God rejoices to enter that temple which is their heart, as much as they rejoice to stand in the temple of Jerusalem.

At the Last Supper, Jesus again speaks about this joyful mission given to him to reveal his Father's love to simple people. He looks around at his twelve friends. Do not glamorise these men.They were not wearing haloes at that meal. They are as human, weak and broken as we are, as all people are. Jesus looks around at them and prays for them. What does he say in his prayer? 'Father, I have made your name known to them and will continue to make it known, so that the love with which you loved me may be in them, and so that I may be in them' (John 17:26). And we too are included in this prayer. 'Father, I pray not only for these, but for those also who through their words will believe in me' (John 17:20). Surely, what Jesus said elsewhere, that kings and prophets desired to hear these things but did not hear is true.

I was going to say let us put away this very misleading idea of our unworthiness. But I suggest we do something else. Let us explore it more deeply and when we do dig down deep here we can strike a rich vein of gold hiding in this dark idea of unworthiness. I do not deny my unworthiness. I cannot. I accept that I am unworthy. I am totally unworthy but I am still loved in this incredible way by God. It is when I realise that his love has nothing to do with my worthiness, but everything to do with his goodness, that I am on the way to being transformed. He loves me not for what I have or do, but for what I am. And what am I? I am his. He loves me because I am his, as a young mother loves her newborn baby, not for what it can do for her, but simply because the baby is hers, is part of her.

> Do not be afraid, for I have redeemed you;
> I have called you by your name, you are mine.
> *Isaiah 43:2*

We could put it this way. The notion of being unworthy can come either from Satan or from the Holy Spirit. When it comes from Satan it brings upset and discouragement. When Satan reminds us of our unworthiness, he gives it an ugly twist. His suggestion goes like this: 'You are unworthy (which is true!). But it's your own fault. You could be worthy (which is false!). If you were a better person and more faithful to God you could be worthy of the love he offers' (i.e. you could be worthy by your own efforts – which is totally false!). When the thought of unworthiness comes from the Holy Spirit it floods us with immense joy and gratitude and can even lead to tears. The Spirit says, 'You are unworthy and nothing you can ever do can make you worthy of receiving God's love, but God is in love with you the way you are and offers you, as you are now, the embrace of his unconditional love.'

And so the very concept of my unworthiness, which seemed to be the great stumbling-block to enjoying God's love and power, can become the springboard into new life, new wonder and deep joy which no person or thing can take from me, because it doesn't depend on any person or thing, but only on the faithful love of God who says, 'For the mountains may depart, the hills be shaken, but my love for you will never leave you' (Isaiah 54:10). The place of my unworthiness where I can feel so hopeless and help-less, that dark place can lead me on like a tunnel out into the light, into open space, into joy and celebration.

When this truth sinks in, then I am hearing the good news with my heart. I am not just hearing sounds with my ears but I hear the meaning with my heart. Surely this was why the people who listened to Jesus hung on his words, even forgot about food and said to one another, 'No one ever spoke like this man'. Those people, just like you and me, knew they were hearing Truth itself speak. Their own inner spirit, which was good and true because made in God's image, echoed Jesus' words. 'God dresses the flow-ers and feeds the birds. Are you not more precious?' When he said it they knew that they were. Jesus loves these peo-ple. He comes to them because he loves them. He comes to tell them they are loved by the Father because they belong to the Father, not because of any worthiness. He knows our human hearts have difficulty in understanding uncon-ditional love. Can we not see that it is precisely because we are helpless, broken sinners, and because we feel unwor-thy that he comes with this good news? He comes himself with the news because we could not have believed it if anyone less than God told us. Coming from any other than God the news would have been too good to be true.

50

Isaiah, in a beautiful passage, describes God inviting us to come and be nourished and refreshed by his word of love:

> Oh, come to the water all you who are thirsty;
> though you have no money, come!
> Buy corn without money, and eat,
> and, at no cost, wine and milk.
> *Isaiah 55:1*

Why are we invited? Because we are thirsty and hungry, because we need love and healing. It is not because we have money and can pay. It is our very thirst and hunger that guarantee that we shall be nourished and refreshed. Our wounds are our chief claim to healing. All we have to do is 'come', 'drink', 'eat'. And the prophet knows that God's living word will not fail in its task. 'Yes, as the rain and the snow come down from the heavens and do not return without watering the earth, making it yield and giving growth to provide seed for the sower and bread for the eating, so the word that goes from my mouth does not return to me empty, without carrying out my will and succeeding in what it was sent to do' (Isaiah 55:10).

Look at the love between the rain and the earth. It is only when they are united in love that the earth can bear fruit. The earth alone, without the rain, will remain barren. The rain looking down on the earth does not say, 'When you, dry earth, become fresh and green and fruitful, I shall fall upon you as a reward.' The good rain knows the earth cannot become fruitful unless it falls upon it in love. Our good God knows we cannot be fruitful without him. He does not say, 'When you begin to be fruitful in loving one another I will come to reward you.' We cannot love one another without him. It is our very dryness and hardness that draw him to us.

God's unconditional love softens our hearts and enables us to grow. True love is that which is given, not because we are worthy or have earned it, but because we need it. It is given, not in the hope of receiving anything in return, but simply because it is the very nature of love to give itself. And while we often fail to love like that, still, our deep-down good self tells us that this is true and that such love is possible for us. Our deepest self is made in the image of the God who loves unconditionally. That is why we can believe in it and also believe, despite our failures, that it is possible for us. When we meet this kind of love in others, our hearts can be transformed. Here is a story:

In the desert there lived a saintly hermit called Anthony. All who came to ask his prayers and guidance were struck by the deep peace of the cave where he lived. One evening a wandering preacher came by and asked for hospitality for the night. Anthony received him graciously and, after sharing his food with him, invited the visitor to join him in evening prayer. Anthony opened a box and took out his most precious possession, a book of the Holy Scripture. It was beautifully bound and decorated. This was Anthony's one and only treasure. As they prayed, the preacher looked at the book and could see it was something special and clearly very valuable. He was tempted. Greed entered his heart and, that night, as Anthony slept, the preacher stole the book and left. He went to a nearby town, found a merchant and offered him the book for twenty gold coins. The merchant asked for time so he could consult an expert about its value. The preacher reluctantly agreed to return the next day. The merchant then went to the desert to consult Anthony who, he felt sure, would know the value of the holy book. He reached the cave and showed Anthony the book and explained that a man wanted to sell it for twenty gold coins, but he was not sure if it was worth that much.

Anthony looked at his own precious book and said it was indeed worth that much. The merchant thanked him and left. When the preacher returned next day, the merchant said he would buy the book. The preacher, out of curiosity, asked how he knew its value. The merchant said he had consulted a holy hermit called Anthony who knew the value of such objects. The preacher was stunned. 'You consulted Anthony!' he exclaimed, 'Yes', said the merchant. 'And what did he say?' asked the preacher. 'I told you' said the merchant, 'he said it was worth twenty gold coins'. 'Yes, I heard you, but what else did he say when he saw the book?' shouted the preacher. 'He said nothing', replied the merchant, 'he handled it rather fondly and simply said it was worth the money, so now we can close the deal.' By now, the preacher, visibly upset and disturbed cried out, 'No! Give me back the book. I've changed my mind.' He took the book and, in confusion and repentance of heart, hurried back to Anthony's cave. He entered with great new reverence and respect, threw himself at Anthony's feet, begged forgiveness and asked to be accepted as his disciple.

9

DON'T CHANGE, GROW

The rain falls on the dry earth and makes it blossom. It comes because is needed. It does not wait for the earth to change. During Advent we pray that the heavens may open and that the Lord may come upon us like spring rain. This he does, coming to us as we are, not waiting for us to change. Indeed, he does not even come to change us. It may seem strange to say that God does not come to change us. But when you think of it, true love must be like that. In a way it's obvious. If I say to you, 'I love you and I want to change you to be better or different', this is a contradiction. It means, in fact, that I do not love *you*. I love some image of you, some other version of you which I have created. If I desire to change somebody, I do not really love that person. If you accept someone on condition that they change, that they be different, then in fact you are not accepting them. The only real love is unconditional love which is God's kind of loving.

In saying we should not try to change people, we are not saying that we must pretend there is no evil in the person. There is evil in every person, evil in me, in you. Eyes of love will not be blind to the evil, but they will see much more. Love will see past the evil to the real you. Love will not identify you with the evil in you. In the presence of love, which is also truth, you and I will not be led into any hypocrisy or pretence about evil. I believe that there will remain a real sense of the existence of evil. Indeed, I believe there will be an even sharper awareness of that evil in the presence of true love, but simultaneously there will be an awareness of something greater, something overwhelmingly greater which robs the awareness of evil of its sting, of its power to demolish me. I will realise that the love is greater, that I am still totally accepted, even as I am. A healing takes place in that moment. This helps me to understand the saints. They

54

had both these insights at the same moment, an acute awareness of sin and a joyful certainty of loving acceptance. This
resulted for many of them in tears, the tears of Magdalen.
These are tears not of sadness but of great wonder and joy.

Jesus loves in this way. Isn't it wonderful that Jesus, the
only one who has a right to put a condition on love, puts
none. Jesus, the only one qualified to judge, does not judge.
Jesus, the only one free from cooperation with evil, does not
let his eye stay on our evil, but goes past it to the good of our
deepest selves. In the gospel story it was Simon the Pharisee
who was saying to himself, 'If this man were a prophet, he
would know who this woman is that is touching him and
what a bad name she has' (Luke 7:39). Simon is so conscious
of Magdalen's sins he can see nothing else. It is Jesus who is
aware of her love. Have you noticed that in the story of the
prodigal son it is only the elder brother who speaks about
the evil in his young brother? It is he who rants about the
disgrace, the waste of money, the prostitution. The father
makes no mention of the young lad's failure. The father is
love. Notice also that when the Father ran down the road to
welcome the young son, he embraced him in his rags of sin.
He did not wait for the boy to have a shower and change
into the best robe!

God can cope with us exactly as we are. Maybe it's because
he alone sees us exactly as we are. Looking at us with eyes of
love he sees more than we see. 'God does not see as man
sees; man looks at appearances but Yahweh looks at the
heart' (1 Samuel 16:7). We judge ourselves and each other.
God does not. God simply loves. And he loves with his
whole heart and being, as he has asked us to love. This love
of his does not grow. It cannot, because he loves with his
whole heart. I will never be more acceptable to God than I
am right now, whether I am in the depth of sin or the height
of sanctity. His love will not grow. All that can grow is my
awareness of the mystery of that love. It is when I accept that
mystery that, hopefully, my love for him may start to grow.
Here is a lovely word from Charles de Foucauld. 'To love

anyone is to hope in him for always. From the moment at which we begin to judge anyone, to limit our confidence in him, from the moment at which we identify him with what we know of him and so reduce him to that, we cease to love him and he ceases to be able to be better'. Jesus would say Amen to that.

God comes to us in Jesus because he sees our beauty which, unfortunately, is often hidden and obscured by sin and evil. He comes to reveal that beauty. He wants to help us dig in the field of our lives and uncover the treasure buried there. He knows that if we glimpse that treasure, then we might be ready to sell all to keep it. Our deep, hidden selves, made in God's image, are treasure that all the money in the world could not buy. One day Jesus was teaching those simple, humble, broken people who flocked to hear him. He put a question to them: 'What, then, will a man gain if he wins the whole world and ruins his life? Or what has a man to offer in exchange for his life?' (Matthew 16:26). I always used to read these words as a kind of warning, as if Jesus were saying, 'Don't risk hell for all the money in the world; don't sell your soul for pleasure or money and risk exchanging heaven for hell, that would be a bad bargain.' This meaning is still there, but I now find other rich meaning in these words. Jesus is asking us to see the wonder and mystery of our own beings. He wants us to reflect on our own beauty, value, worth. So he is asking these people whom he loves, 'What would you exchange for your own self? What value do you put on yourself? Do you think the wealth of the whole world would be enough to buy you?' We can imagine Jesus looking around at the faces of those listeners. He speaks with such sincerity and power. 'If you put yourself in one scale of the balance and put all the riches of the world in the other scale, then the balance will tip in your favour. You are worth more than the world and if you sold yourself even for the whole world, it would be a bad bargain.' And the listeners knew he meant it and they knew it was true.

Jesus says the same to you and me now. He comes to

reveal my own inmost self, the deeper beauty, the hidden treasure. It is when I listen and believe and agree with what he tells me about myself that I begin to live and grow. Jesus does not come to change me but to invite me to grow. This growth happens when I accept his love for me as I am. He invites me to become more and more my true self. I cannot grow and become myself until I first accept myself with his acceptance of me. Paul says if our hidden self is to grow it must be 'planted in love' (Ephesians 3:17).

Notice that I reject the word 'change' and choose the word 'grow'. Change can suggest becoming someone else. Growth suggests plan, direction. We say a seed 'grows'. We do not say it 'changes', even though a fantastic change takes place. The seed grows and brings forth all the wonder of the shape, design, colour and perfume of the flower that is already hidden within it. All this beauty is already there potentially and the gardener 'sees' it because he looks with loving eyes. Jesus says in one parable, 'My Father is the gardener' (John 15:1).

So when Jesus met the sinners, he did not scold or lecture them about sin. He did not even make them aware of their sin. Most of them were already depressingly aware of their sins. He moved with them in genuine acceptance and this friendship touched new springs of growth. And when he rose from the dead, he remained the same compassionate, understanding friend. When he came back to his friends after the resurrection we can imagine how miserable and ashamed they must have been, yet we do not find any sense of guilt, but rather total joy and deep peace. Why? Because Jesus took them as he found them. His love always gives what we need, not what we deserve. These friends needed encouragement and healing. So there was no scolding. He did not ask them where were they last Friday! Indeed he made no reference to his terrible ordeal, the kind of thing we would do to arouse guilt in a friend who had let us down. It is the same Risen Lord who comes to us now, accepting us as he finds us.

10

THE GOOD SAMARITAN

Let us set ourselves to know Yahweh;
that he will come is as certain as the dawn,
he will come to us as showers come,
like spring rains watering the earth.
Hosea 6:3

The prophet Hosea here affirms what we have been saying. Our God is one who comes to us. He comes to us just as we are, because we belong to him and he knows we need him. His coming is always very gentle because he knows we are fragile. He comes like spring rain to make us fruitful. He comes to help us discover our own true selves. It is this very precious self that he visits.

I do not have to change and become someone else to receive him and experience his nourishing love. Isaiah reflects on this when he says:

Let the wilderness and the dry-lands exult,
let the wasteland rejoice and bloom,
let it bring forth flowers like the jonquil,
let it rejoice and sing for joy.
Isaiah 35:1-2

Notice that it is the very wasteland, the very desert that will bloom: The Lord does not say: 'You must move house, you must move elsewhere so that we can make a beautiful garden.' No! He says: 'Let us work on this apparent wasteland, the desert of your poor dry heart.' To this dry heart he sends the refreshing spring rain of his love. He sees the seeds there waiting for his gentle touch. This desert place will be covered with waving, golden daffodils.

It does not mean that God ignores the sin and evil in me. Even that he can reveal to me without making me feel crushed with shame and guilt. Again the touch is gentle. He sees these sins as wounds needing healing. Hosea says: 'He will heal us; he will bandage our wounds' (Hosea 6:2). Our sin and failure lose their sting and poison as he bends over us to pour in oil and balm and bandage the wounds. When he was accused by self-righteous men of taking sin too lightly, Jesus defended himself by saying: 'It is not those who are well who need the doctor, but the sick' (Luke 5:32). He has come to bandage our wounds. This coming is always gentle, always healing. Its fruit is peace. A lovely verse from an anonymous fifteenth-century poet tells us how we will recognise the presence of the Lord:

> Thou shalt know him when he comes
> Not by any din of drums
> Nor by the vantage of his airs
> Nor by anything he wears
> Neither by his crown
> Nor his gown.
> For his presence known shall be
> by the holy harmony
> that his coming makes in thee.

It is the sick who need the doctor. It is the hurt and wounded traveller by the roadside who needs a good Samaritan. Jesus himself is the first Good Samaritan. The point about the story of the Good Samaritan is that it does not follow reason or logic. In the story the unfortunate victim who had been mugged and robbed was a Jew. As he lay there helpless, he could reasonably have hoped for help from the first two people to come along. They were fellow Jews and professional religious, people who had reason to help. But they passed by. Then came a Samaritan, the one who had best reason for passing by. The fierce enmity between Jew and Samaritan was known to all. At the end of the story, when Jesus asks his questioner, a Jewish lawyer, which of the three was the neighbour, the lawyer will not even say the word 'Samaritan'. He answers, 'The one who took pity on him' (Luke 10:37). In the story then, contrary to all reason, it is the Samaritan who helps. The truth is that we are talking here about something more elevated than reason. The Samaritan helps the wounded Jew not because it is the reasonable thing to do, but because it is the loving thing to do. He is moved not by reason, but by pity. 'But a Samaritan traveller who came upon him was moved with compassion when he saw him. He went up and bandaged his wounds, pouring oil and wine on them' (Luke 10:33-34).

On one occasion, the enemies of Jesus, wishing to insult him, called him a madman, a Samaritan (John 8:48). Little did they know how close they were to the truth. For Jesus is the original Good Samaritan. He saw us lying by the wayside of life, attacked and wounded by fear, guilt, sin, doubt and self-hatred. We lay bleeding, powerless, with no one to help us. He saw self-righteous people hurry by, busy about so-called religious duties. And he was moved to pity and came and knelt right down there on the road beside us. He poured the soothing balm of love over our wounds, bandaged us, lifted us up and carried us to a safe place and paid for our upkeep and further healing. He paid not a few coins, but his own precious blood. You see, our sufferings have power to move our God to compassion, as the suffering of the prodigal son moved first the father's heart and then his whole person. And remember that the young lad brought his sufferings on himself. The Good Samaritan reminds us of the Good Shepherd. He goes out into dangerous wild places after a silly stray sheep. When he finds it, there is no scolding, kicking or beating. He takes it joyfully on his shoulders and carries it to safety. Our 'reasonable' charity does not cover this kind of behaviour. God acts out of love and love has no limits, no rules.

We find the very same gentleness and healing love in Jesus after the resurrection. See him again, the Good Samaritan on the road to Emmaus, as he joins two very hurt disciples. These two men are wounded by disappointment, by shame, by fear. Jesus joins them on the way. He need not have done so. He walks at their pace. He asks why they are so sad. Gently he opens their eyes to the wonder of all that had happened. How did these two men describe their experience? They said, 'Did not our hearts burn within us as he talked to us on the road?' (Luke 24:32). They did not say, 'Then we clearly understood with our minds.' No! Their hearts were burning. God pours out love, 'a full measure, pressed down, shaken together, and running over' (Luke 6:38). God is so extravagant we are almost shocked! Indeed we have always had religious people who seem to feel it their duty to keep God's generosity within reasonable bounds! Karl Rahner has an apt comment on this. He writes, 'Some theologians seem to think that grace would not be grace if God was too liberal with it.'

Maybe one subtle reason why we are almost shocked by the extravagance of God's love is that deep within us we know we are called to be like him in whose image and likeness we are created. The prophet says, 'Be holy, for I, Yahweh your God, am holy' (Leviticus 19:2). And Jesus tells us to be like our heavenly Father. These words seem to propose an impossible ideal. Yet, if we explore them, we will find in these very words a gleam of hope that what we are called to is not impossible but is our very deepest fulfilment. Notice that God does not put his invitation to holiness in the context of reward and punishment. He does not say, 'Be holy, be like your father and, if you are, I will reward you, but if you are not, I will punish you.' He says something quite different. He says, 'Be holy, for I, your God, am holy.' 'Be like your Father.' The primary communication here is 'Remember who you are, you belong to me. I am your God. I am your Father. You are part of the family. You have received the Holy Spirit of our family. You can be holy.'

And the first-born in our family, Jesus Christ, shows us that it is possible. Often not easy, but possible. And, even more, as we have said, he offers us power to live and love like him. It is possible if we live and abide in the love of that Saviour.

11

GOD'S KIND OF HOLINESS

'The mind is like a parachute. It works better when it is open.' These homely words of wisdom have great force when we think of the mind's search to understand God. God is infinite mystery. The human mind cannot comprehend him, but it is made to search for him with its companion, the heart. In this search it must always remain open to wonder and surprise. Paul prays that we may come to know the 'love of Christ, which is beyond all knowledge' (Ephesians 3:19). The Psalmist ponders the mystery of God's love present and active in every place and time and exclaims, 'Such knowledge is beyond my understanding' (Psalm 139:6). We should explore the mystery of God with a sense of wonder and excitement and deep, worshipping humility.

One problem is that we think we know what God is like. We transfer our knowledge of ourselves and our emotions to God. Of course we keep saying that in God these emotions are infinitely great. But even as we use the expression 'infinitely great', we are still bound by our human imagination and are probably trying to imagine an object of immense size or a distance beyond the horizon. The saints say that what we know about God is more untrue than true. It must be so. This humbles us but it also liberates us. It can protect us from fashioning a kind of idol, a small God of our own making. In a sense we are more at ease with a small God, one we can manage and predict.

'Be holy, for I, Yahweh your God, am holy' (Leviticus 19:2). We have already looked at these words and noticed how we almost instinctively recoil from them since they appear to propose an impossible challenge. We are called to be holy as God is holy. What can this mean? Let us now, with a new, open, humble attitude approach this attribute of God, his holiness. Let us ask Jesus to be our teacher. Let us put away our preconceived ideas of holiness and allow Jesus to teach us.

I am sure we all have our ideas of what it means to be holy. The word is much used in Scripture, in prayer and liturgy. In the Gloria of the Mass we say, 'You alone are Holy' and at the Preface we join with the heavenly choir to sing out 'Holy, Holy, Holy, Lord God of hosts.' When we use the words 'holy' or 'holiness', we usually think of distance, especially distance from ourselves in our unholiness. We think of height and separation – God is above us. We think of great purity, glory, total perfection. When we transfer the word 'holy' to people, it becomes more ambiguous but still suggests distance and separation. It suggests someone much better than ourselves, someone who has overcome sin, the popular idea of the saint. I am not here thinking of the phoney 'holy person'. Fortunately, most people can spot this caricature of the genuine article. But still the call remains; we are all asked to be holy as our God is holy. We turn to Jesus to learn what this could mean for us.

As always, Jesus is full of surprises. He turns many of our ideas upside down. For us 'holiness' suggests separation and distance. Yet this Jesus, who is himself the holiness of God and our holiness, comes close, closer than we could ever have imagined or hoped for. In the Old Testament Moses exclaimed, 'What great nation is there that has its gods so near as Yahweh our God is to us?' (Deuteronomy 4:7). And Moses did not know about the Incarnation or the Eucharist. A Messiah was expected by the chosen people. He would be God's Holy One. Where would he be found when he came? With our idea of holiness, we would expect to find him in some holy place, a separated place, away from the contagion of sin, a lofty mountain, perhaps, or a consecrated temple. In fact, our Jesus is born at the side of the road. All are equal and welcome at the side of the road. There are no doors, no gates, no dogs, no burglar alarms in Bethlehem's cave. But this cave is now a holy place because he is there. And when his time to die comes, he dies at the side of the road. Passers-by can stop and look and many did. And now this Calvary is forever a holy place because he died there. Indeed, God comes very close and we have to revise our strange idea that holiness suggests distance and separation.

But there is a much more meaningful closeness that our poor hearts crave for. We wonder, will he come close to me, the real me, so weak and so ashamed of my failures? Would he come very near to me, to my heart, if he knew me, really knew me? Would he want to have me as a friend? This is the cry of our heart that our God really understands. Indeed, it is this secret cry that brought him down so close that he would want to make this poor heart his dwelling-place. And so it happens. Jesus tells us that if anyone tries to keep his word, 'my Father will love him, and we shall come to him and make our home with him' (John 14:23). And now, as the cave of Bethlehem and the hill of Calvary were made forever holy by his resting there, so our hearts become holy.

They say that one day in heaven God was very tired and felt he needed a little break. He decided to take a long weekend, but didn't know where to find a quiet place where he wouldn't be disturbed. He called some wise counsellors and asked for suggestions. The first counsellor suggested that the top of the highest mountain would surely be quiet and undisturbed. But God reminded him that believers often climb the highest peaks precisely to get in touch with God! Another counsellor suggested the moon as a safe retreat. God reminded him that they were in the twentieth century and the moon was no longer safe. Finally, one wise counsellor said, 'I know the perfect hiding place, Lord. You can hide in the human heart. They will never think of looking for you there!'

True. We do not expect God to come to our poor hearts. But Jesus is the God of surprises and he comes that close. And if we magnify our sins and unworthiness and feel he would not come that close, he goes out of his way to assure us. Let us recall how he does this in the first great public act of his human life among us, his baptism in the Jordan. Imagine the river Jordan on that day. See the excited crowds, the tents where people are camping, the groups sitting round fires chatting. Every sort of person is here: country folk, town dwellers, farmers, traders, soldiers, young, old, even some Scribes and Pharisees. What is the attraction? It is a man of mystery with powerful words that can shake the human heart. He is called the Baptist. He has emerged from the desert, an ascetic figure who scorns normal food and dress. He is a man on fire and he forces you to listen.

What is this man saying? He speaks of a new age about to dawn. The long-awaited Messiah will soon appear. People should be ready. He will be the Holy One who will not tolerate sin. He will carry an axe and will cut down all barren and rotten trees. He will carry a great winnowing fan and will separate the chaff from the grain, the bad from the good. Get ready to meet him. Confess your unholiness and, as a sign that you wish to be clean enough to meet him, enter this river to be baptised, washed and made clean.

Then one day the God of surprises appears. Jesus walks along the river bank, unknown and unnoticed. He has come some distance and is tired. He sits with one of the groups round a fire and is offered a drink. After a spell of resting and chatting, he stands up and moves towards the river, greeting folk on the way. Then he joins the line of people making their way into the river for baptism. Slowly he makes his way down into the water, keeping his place in the queue. He looks at the back, head and shoulders of the man in front of him. The woman in the line behind him looks at his back and shoulders. They move slowly forward. John is busy pouring the water and shouting words of encouragement. He must be rightly happy with the response to his preaching.

John pours the water on the man in front of Jesus and then looks up. His eyes meet those of Jesus and the Holy Spirit enlightens his heart that this is the Messiah. It would be hard to find words to describe John's emotions. His heart is full of conflicting thoughts. Not only did his preaching not apply to this man, but this man should not be in the river! John has been preparing sinners to meet this man so that they may be made righteous by him. Also, John is aware of his own sinfulness and knows that he too needs the baptism and salvation which this man brings. John tries to dissuade him. 'It is I who need baptism from you' he says, 'and yet you come to me!' (Matthew 3:14).

Poor John! He is the official herald of the Messiah, the God-chosen and appointed messenger sent to prepare the way. And now he who will call himself 'the Way' stands humbly with sinners asking for baptism. John is involved in a mystery and just now cannot cope. John will have to reorganise his theology, his understanding of God, of sin, of mercy, just as Peter and Paul — and so many others later on, and you and I today — will have to let go our narrow and miserable ideas of God and let God himself teach us. John the Baptist and all of us will have to find a new definition of holiness.

To be holy is to come near, to come close, even as close as the very broken heart of man and woman. To that motley crew at the Jordan – and surely every type of person must have been there – Jesus is saying, 'I will not separate myself from you. And I will not separate you from one another. My cousin John is right when he says I am coming to destroy evil, but I will do it in a new way, my Father's way. I have forgotten my axe and my winnowing fan! I do not wish to separate you from God or from each other. Rather the opposite. I wish to draw you all close to my Father who is your Father and to draw you close to each other. I will not separate the good from the bad, but I hope to open the eyes of all to see how much good there is in the so-called bad and how the goodness of the good is my Father's gift.'

John still has surprises ahead. Moved by the Spirit he baptises the Lord and receives a revelation from the Father that this is in fact the Beloved Son. All is in order, even if John does not understand. God actually knows what he is doing! This must have been a help to John, but, as things turn out, John is still baffled and even doubting. After the baptism John expects Jesus to take over and begin baptising with the Spirit. But no. Jesus slips off into the desert to pray and fast. Though why Jesus should need to fast is another mystery! Then, after his time in the desert, Jesus emerges into public life and moves around the towns and villages, preaching the good news of God's love, fraternising with sinners and healing the sick.

Meanwhile, John had been put in prison by Herod for criticising the king's marriage to his brother's wife. From prison, John follows the progress of Jesus and is again upset and confused by what he hears. Jesus has not yet started separating the good from the bad. Indeed he does not seem to be able to distinguish good from bad! He is so often with sinners that he has been nicknamed 'friend of sinners'. Nor does Jesus stay in one place by the Jordan or the lake to await sinners coming for baptism. He goes round to meet them in case they might be too shy to come to the river. John in prison has a crisis of doubt and sends messengers to Jesus to ask him, 'Are you the one who is to come, or have we got to wait for someone else?' (Matthew 11:3).

If we are sometimes slow to understand God and his ways, let us take heart here. If John, the chosen messenger, this John of whom Jesus said, 'I tell you solemnly, of all the children born of women, a greater than John the Baptist has never been seen' (Matthew 11:11), if this man was confused and doubting, must we not be more patient and humble in our efforts to understand and follow God? At the same time, let us greatly rejoice in the answer Jesus gave to John's question, 'Are you the one who is to come?' Jesus answered, 'Go back and tell John what you hear and see;

the blind see again and the lame walk, lepers are cleansed, and the deaf hear, and the dead are raised to life and the Good News is proclaimed to the poor; and happy is the man who does not lose faith in me' (Matthew 11:4-6). God's holiness is God's compassionate closeness to us in all our brokenness. We do not have to wait for another. Advent is over. God is among us, 'presente' in Jesus.

12

RECONCILIATION

God's holiness brings him close to us. It is a false holiness that separates and creates distance between us and God and between one another. This was the false, phoney 'holiness' of the Pharisees. The very name Pharisee means 'separated one'. Jesus warned against this kind of holiness: 'If your virtue goes no deeper than that of the scribes and Pharisees, you will never get into the kingdom of heaven' (Matthew 5:20). The holiness of God brought God close to us in Jesus. He came in compassion to heal and renew, not to condemn, but to save. He came 'not to be served, but to serve' (Matthew 20:28). This is genuine holiness, real greatness, true divinity. All our inclinations are in the opposite direction.

Consider the phenomenon of the personality cult. I believe this phenomenon reveals our terribly impoverished idea of what constitutes greatness, even divinity. It is instructive to watch what happens when people rise to great public fame. The more famous the person becomes, the more distant he or she is from the ordinary mortal in the street. A person appears with great gifts of leadership in politics or religion, in acting or in sport. The gifts bring acclaim, power, wealth and privilege. Gradually the famous person gets pushed away from ordinary people, is seen differently, is literally less seen. The famous one will travel in dark curtained cars and private jets, will be surrounded by bodyguards and have look-alikes to decoy fans or enemies. When seen, this rising star walks in a kind of glory. As this star gets pushed away from ordinary people and activities, there may be an occasional descent to earth and we all marvel as the media give us an exclusive shot of one of these 'immortals' holding a shovel or pouring a cup of tea or embracing a baby! This is meant to provoke admiration and wonder that such a 'great' should come so close and engage in such humble human activity.

What is happening? The person is becoming godlike within our idea of divinity – distant, out-of-touch, free from suffering, having immense wealth, power, influence. And we are all involved, the new god or goddess, the media and promoters and we, the worshippers. There is no one innocent enough to say 'the Emperor has no clothes'. Let us thank God for the true God, for Jesus who came to overthrow our infantile and conceited notions of divinity. 'You know that among the pagans the rulers lord it over them, and their great men make their authority felt. This is not to happen among you' (Matthew 20:25-26). Maybe this was the original sin, to want to be godlike, with our idea of what that might mean. Maybe Jesus is the supreme irony, inviting us to be like God in the true sense. God could have been smiling when he said, 'Be holy, for I, Yahweh your God, am holy' (Leviticus 19:2). Jesus knew he was proposing something difficult when he said, 'Be perfect just as your heavenly Father is perfect' (Matthew 5:48). But in truth, it is perhaps more difficult than we realised, because in asking us to be godlike he is asking us to come close to each other in compassion and self-emptying love.

But this very self-emptying, unselfish love for each other is possible precisely because God is his kind of God and not our kind. The true God is close, is with us, is for us, is on our side offering us power to love, to break down all the barriers we erect between ourselves and God and between each other. God in true holiness comes close in Jesus to enable us to become holy with a holiness which will show itself in destroying the distance between us, in making us one, in healing the wounds of division and enabling us to forgive one another. The scripture word for this is 'reconciliation'.

Here are some words from St Paul on this: 'For anyone who is in Christ, there is a new creation; the old creation has gone, and now the new one is here. It is all God's work. It was God who reconciled us to himself through Christ and gave us the work of handing on this reconciliation. God in Christ was reconciling the world to himself, not holding men's faults against them' (2 Corinthians 5:17-19). Jesus is among us, restoring the old harmony between God and his people and between people themselves. God, who is love, keeps no record of wrong, he does not hold our faults against us. Paul begs us not to neglect this healing gift from God offered in Jesus, 'The appeal that we make in Christ's name is: be reconciled to God' (2 Corinthians 5:20). God has done his bit by coming close to us in Jesus. We must do our bit and come close to him and accept the gift of reconciliation he offers. There are three components involved in being reconciled. There is my sin which separates me from God and my neighbour. There is God's offer of forgiveness and healing in Jesus and there is my acceptance of the healing and forgiveness. Only one of these elements presents a problem; the third, my acceptance of healing and forgiveness.

I must say yes. I must accept the gift and trust this God who is so close, trust that he does forgive and forget and that he really does give me the power to forgive others. I must let go the evil, the sin, to experience freedom and peace. I must forgive myself. I must go in with my Father and celebrate like the prodigal son. The alternative is to magnify the sin, hang on to guilt and judgment of myself and others and thus exclude myself from the celebration.

In Sri Lanka young boys catch monkeys in the forest to sell them as pets in the market-place. To capture the wild creatures they go to a place in the forest where they know the monkeys play in the trees above. They ignore the monkeys and begin to play with a hollowed-out coconut shell. They have made a small opening in the shell and have put a stone inside. The boys play with the shell as a rattle, knowing that the curious monkeys are peering down from the branches above. After a while they leave the shell on the ground and hide in the bushes. They have tied a string around the shell and hold the end of the string in their hiding place. Soon the chattering monkeys descend, pick up the plaything and rattle it in imitation of the boys: Then, urged by curiosity, a monkey puts his paw into the shell to investigate the source of the rattle. He grasps the stone inside and tries to remove it. The hole is big enough for his paw to fit in, but now that the paw is clenched to hold the stone, it cannot come out. The boys behind the bush pull the string and drag the screeching monkey towards them. All the monkey has to do to be free is to let go the stone, open his paw, pull it out and race to the freedom of the trees. But this he will not do. He wants that stone. He will not let go and ends up in a cage.

Do we not hold on to things, even very trivial things, and lose the freedom Jesus offers? It could be something between God and me, something that happened long ago for which I blamed God, some failure, some loss, a bereavement. Or it might be something between myself and another person, a quarrel, a deception, an insult. Even after many years, I hold on to a memory, some mind picture, a look, a sneer, a tone of voice. I hold on and am imprisoned by such things. Jesus invites me to let go, to be reconciled, to become a new creation. He does more than invite. He offers the necessary power. Paul reminds us that it is all God's work. Of course we can expect to hear another voice whispering to us to hold on. 'It was not your fault. You have your pride. You already made an approach and were spurned etc. . .' We all know this voice. Hold on. But if we hold on and don't let go, we end up in a cage. We can let go, we can be free. Not by our own power. If we could manage by our own power, why did Jesus come?

But Jesus has come and is with us, offering us the freedom of the children of God. He himself says, 'If the Son makes you free, you will be free indeed' (John 8:36). He came to set prisoners free. The worst kind of prison is the one we build around ourselves. Some years ago, I conducted a retreat for a group from Zambia's university in Lusaka. In a reconciliation service we prayed for each other to receive the power to let go any anger we might have against those who had hurt us in the past. Later in the day, one of the group, a lecturer from another African country, came to me in great joy to share a blessing he had received. He first told me of the painful circumstances that had forced him out of his own native country in West Africa. Years before, in his own country, at a time of political upset, he was falsely accused of being involved in an attempted coup and was imprisoned. He knew the person responsible for the accusation. After some time he was released from prison but was exiled from his native land. Since then he had carried anger and hatred in his heart against his accuser. During the reconciliation service he felt empowered to surrender this anger and forgive the man responsible for his suffering. He did so and experienced great freedom and peace. This was how he described it to me. 'Although I had been physically released for years from prison, I was not really a free man. I was still a prisoner in a prison of my own making. My heart was a prisoner of anger and hate and this prison I brought with me wherever I went. Today with God's help I have forgiven this man and today, for the first time, I feel completely free. I am no longer a prisoner.'

Jesus came to set us free, to liberate us from all traps, prisons and cages, and to fulfil the beautiful words of the Psalmist:

> Blessed be Yahweh who did not let us fall
> a victim to those teeth,
> who let us escape like birds
> from the fowler's net.
> He tore the net
> and we escaped.
> *Psalm 124:6-7*

13

INNER PEACE

The healing power of God's gift of reconciliation must touch the three great relationships in our lives: our relationship with God, with each other and with our own selves. These three areas are all wounded by sin. In each there can be disharmony and alienation which cry out for healing. In Christian preaching the emphasis is usually placed on the need to be reconciled to God and to our neighbour. But, in fact, the first and most basic and painful form of alienation we experience is alienation within ourselves. Reconciliation with God and my neighbour is intimately related to being reconciled with my own self. If we do not enjoy some inner peace, harmony and love, it will be quite difficult to approach others in forgiveness and love. The first and most important reconciliation must take place within myself. When that happens we become whole. We are healthy as people. They say that the words 'holy', 'health' and 'whole' are all related and come from one root. It is easy to believe that.

'Be holy, for I, Yahweh your God, am holy' (Leviticus 19:2). This God has revealed himself as Trinity, the Holy Trinity of Father, Son and Spirit bound together in a community of love, a holy harmony. So we can say the call to be like God is an invitation to harmony within ourselves. It begins with joyful acceptance of God's first gift to us, the gift of our own selves. It invites me to pray with the Psalmist:

> It was you who created my inmost self,
> and put me together in my mother's womb;
> For all these mysteries I thank you:
> for the wonder of myself.
> *Psalm 139:13-14*

Let me stop wishing I was someone else, stop comparing myself with others, stop judging myself. Let me go further

and accept that this self is in some strange way wounded
and capable of evil. And go further still and believe that
God knows this and still draws close, very close in love,
with power to heal these wounds, to forgive actual failures, no matter how many or how terrible, and to reach
down to the mysterious roots of the evil with the healing
balm of love. He does not hold my sins against me. He
keeps no record of wrong. He offers a healing so powerful
that I can become a new creation. My part is to believe this
good news and to accept, to see myself as he sees me, to
believe what he tells me about myself, to let go of self-
hatred and self-judgment. My heavenly Father invites me
to go in with him to celebrate this experience of being
found after being lost. We judge ourselves more severely
than God does. If our conscience judges us, St John tells us,
'God is greater than our conscience' (l John 3:20).

We find it so hard to let God be God. We measure him
and impose limits on him and his healing power. We say
'What's done cannot be undone'. With God that is not true.
It is another of our limited human concepts. It is human
wisdom. We speak of the infinite mystery of God's love
revealed in Jesus. A saying attributed to Oscar Wilde goes
like this: 'No man is rich enough to buy back his past.' We
know what he is saying. 'What's done is done and cannot
be undone. Evil is irreversible. You can't gather up spilt
milk.' But this is human wisdom. God can gather up spilt
milk. Christ is rich enough to buy back our past. The very
expression 'buy back' is a common scripture phrase, 'to
redeem'. In Isaiah, the Lord says, 'Do not be afraid, for I
have redeemed you' (Isaiah 43:1).

The holiness of God is the closeness of God and God is
not time-bound. God is loving and healing through all the
three tenses, past, present and future. Make an act of faith
in that healing love which reaches back down your past
life. Enter into that healing river which has been and is
flowing through the whole of your life. Offer for healing
the apparently irreversible evil, the curse you uttered

which seemed to destroy another person, the abortion you advised or caused, the wasting sickness of AIDS brought on by your own careless lifestyle, the hatred towards another which was not healed before the other died, the spiteful calumny which ruined another's good name and which you cannot take back, the hatred towards a father or mother you never met or expect to meet, the apparently unbreakable addiction in which you are trapped and which could have been avoided had you accepted good advice. It is a dreary list and can go on and on. The good news is that there is a power of beauty, truth and love greater than all this misery. There is a healing love available. There are no terminal illnesses of the human spirit.

Yes, you are hurt. You lie wounded by the roadside like that helpless traveller on the road to Jericho. But do not be afraid, take hope. Look up. Someone is approaching. He kneels down beside you. You see the compassion in his eyes. His touch is so gentle as he cleans the wounds with oil and bandages them. And, as he does, so you notice strange scars on his hands. He, too, at some time, must have been attacked and hurt and wounded. Indeed, the prophet says that it is by these very wounds and bruises of his that you are now being healed (Isaiah 53:5). The prophet does not say, 'By his wounds you are judged' or 'By his wounds you are condemned'. No. He says that by his wounds you are healed, because these wounds of his speak of a love beyond telling. There is your healing and reconciliation. 'It is all God's work', says Paul (2 Corinthians 5:18). Let him heal you. And when you remember that evil from the past which seemed irreversible, it will now have lost all power to sting and hurt you. It is healed. Now it can even be a source of joy and of love, for it reminds you of this Good Samaritan. Your healed wounds become like the healed scars on his hands, they remind you of a love you thought impossible.

In Mark's Gospel we have a powerful, dramatic description of a man totally alienated within himself, a man no longer self-possessed but evil-possessed. This is how Mark describes the poor afflicted man:

> A man with an unclean spirit came out from the tombs. The man lived in the tombs and no one could secure him any more, even with a chain; because he had often been secured with fetters and chains but had snapped the chains and broken the fetters, and no one had the strength to control him. All night and all day, among the tombs and in the mountains, he would howl and gash himself with stones.
> *Mark 5:2-6*

What a graphic picture! The man has opted out of life itself. He has chosen to live among the tombs, the place of the dead. He is a man but howls like an animal. He is so alienated within himself that he even hurts himself physically, gashing himself with stones. The evil in him is stronger than any human effort to help him. Some had tried to bind him to prevent him hurting himself, but he broke the fetters. Jesus appears on the scene. 'Catching sight of Jesus from a distance, he ran up and fell at his feet' (v.7). Jesus drives out the evil spirits, and when the terrified onlookers who had run away return, they see the demoniac 'sitting there, clothed and in his full senses' (v.15). Jesus restores the man to himself, to health, to wholeness.

Incidents like this in the life of Jesus drew admiration from many. But in others they provoked a hostile, jealous and bitter criticism. Those who saw in Jesus someone they could not understand, someone who was too different, who would not conform and who challenged traditional structures, these critics put an ugly and sinister interpretation on this kind of healing. 'The man casts out devils only through Beelzebul, the prince of devils' (Matthew 12:24). And so, Jesus, having done battle with an evil spirit, is now confronted by evil with a more human face, people's blind and jealous hatred. He answers them with the parable of the strong man. Very simply he says that evil cannot cast out evil; you cannot put out fire with another fire. The true interpretation of what is happening is that a greater power has now appeared in our world, a power greater than any evil, and it is the power of love, unconditional love. 'If it is through the Spirit of God that I cast devils out, then know that the kingdom of God has overtaken you. How can anyone make his way into a strong man's house and burgle his property unless he has tied up the strong man first?' (Matthew 12:28-29).

This image of 'the kingdom' was central to the teaching of Jesus. Here we have considered one great fruit of the kingdom, the healing of inner alienation and the experience of inner peace and harmony. Again we recall the poem of the fifteenth-century anonymous author,

> Thou shalt know him when he comes
> Not by any din of drums
> Nor by the vantage of his airs
> Nor by anything he wears
> Neither by his crown
> Nor his gown.
> For his presence known shall be
> by the holy harmony
> that his coming makes in thee.

14

GOD AT WORK

When the enemies of Jesus accused him of being in league with Satan and of using evil powers to cast out spirits, he replied, 'If it is through the finger of God that I cast out devils, then know that the kingdom of God has overtaken you' (Luke 11:20). We find this expression, 'kingdom of God' constantly on the lips of Jesus. It is the very heart and centre of his teaching. Jesus did not preach so much about God or himself. He spoke mostly about the kingdom. What did he mean? We have a problem here because we are familiar with the ideas of king and kingdom. We think of a kingdom as a place ruled over by a king. If we are to understand the teaching of Jesus and be enriched and nourished by the fullness of his message, we will have to revise our idea of the reality suggested by the word kingdom.

We can begin by saying we must move away from the idea of kingdom as a place, a land, a territory. When Jesus speaks about the kingdom of God, he is not thinking of a place of perfection where all the people obey God as king and no evil is present. Nor is Jesus primarily thinking of a place of perfection in the next world, populated by angels and saints, where we all hope to go after death. The kingdom of his teaching is not to be indentified with a place either here or in the next world.

What then is it? The kingdom of God among us is the presence of God among us; but not a God sitting on a throne awaiting our worship. It is a very hardworking, active God. The kingdom is not something static, it is a dynamic reality, something that is happening. It is the holiness we spoke of earlier, God's kind of holiness, namely God present and close to us in compassion, blessing, healing, liberating and renewing us. It is the Good Samaritan God kneeling beside us and bandaging our wounds. It is the Good News in action.

We remember how John the Baptist, when he was in prison, began doubting if Jesus was the expected Messiah. John was scandalised by the lifestyle of Jesus. He expected Jesus to stand apart from sinners to denounce sin and separate the good from the bad. John had a narrow idea of the salvation Jesus was bringing and of the richness of the Good News. In his distress and confusion he sent messengers to Jesus to ask, 'Are you the one who is to come, or have we got to wait for someone else?' (Matthew 11:3). This is the reply Jesus gave: 'Go back and tell John what you hear and see; the blind see again, and the lame walk, lepers are cleansed and the deaf hear, and the dead are raised to life and the Good News is proclaimed to the poor; and happy is the man who does not lose faith in me' (Matthew 11:4-5). This is what Jesus meant by the kingdom. God among us. We do not have to wait any more, we do not have to wait for someone else. God is among us in Jesus. We live in *anno domini*.

In his first homily in the synagogue of Nazareth, Jesus chose a passage from Isaiah to describe what he had come to do. This is how he preached:

> The spirit of the Lord has been given to me
> for he has anointed me.
> He has sent me to bring the good news to the poor
> to proclaim liberty to captives
> and to the blind new sight,
> to set the downtrodden free,
> to proclaim the Lord's year of favour.
> *Luke 4:18-19*

And then Jesus added, 'This text is being fulfilled today even as you listen' (Luke 4:22). This is what Jesus means by the kingdom. Notice he describes it as 'news', namely something that is happening now. It is not history, something that happened long ago. It is not prophecy, something that will happen in the future when people turn to

God. No, it is something that is happening today among us. It is God present, healing, loving, re-creating. The kingdom is among us. It is not God outside at a distance urging us to moral improvement. One of God's names is Emmanuel, which means 'God is with us'. He is with us not only in the sense of being present, but with us in the sense of 'for us'. He is saying, 'I am with you all the way'. It is God in Jesus saying 'Presente' when we cry out in pain and confusion asking, 'Lord where are you?'

The kingdom is not a place of perfect people obeying their king. It is people, all right, a great mixture of people, of every kind and type, good and bad, searching for meaning, for happiness, trying to cope with the evil in themselves and the evil from outside. And all the while their king is among them, on their side, encouraging them, nourishing them and strengthening them against the evil. One day, Jesus was challenged by the Scribes and Pharisees for healing a man on the sabbath. They accused him of 'working' on the sabbath. He gave them a simple but profound answer. He said, 'My Father goes on working, and so do I' (John 5:17). We have a working God who never rests from the work of healing and renewing his people. And even when we rest, the kingdom is still happening among us. The Psalmist had this insight. Yahweh 'provides for his beloved as they sleep' (Psalm 127:2). The kingdom is God at work, all the time.

The kingdom is a big fishing-net with good and bad fish. It is a large field with wheat and weeds. It is a seed hidden but growing in a way we cannot understand. It is a spring of water that refreshes and slakes our deepest thirst. It is a mighty tree offering shade to good and bad. It is a chest of treasure buried in our own back garden. It is a piece of yeast, small to the eye but affecting a great mass of dough. It is a gracious king who cancels all debts and invites all from the highways and byways to his banquet table. It is a Father who understands the complex hearts of his children. It is a messenger who says yes to devils when they ask, 'Are you come to destroy us?' Yes, the kingdom has come to destroy all the evil that can threaten God's people.

The kingdom is present in Jesus. It is Jesus among us who, when he sees the suffering of people, does not question Abba, his Father, but does all he can in love to relieve that suffering. He sees sick people but does not say to them, 'This is God's will for you; this is to test you; this is punishment for your sins.' He does not say, 'That's how life is here on earth but there is a better life coming.' He says none of these things. He is, rather, moved to compassion and he heals and consoles and encourages us not to wait for heaven but to try to bring heaven down here to earth by loving and caring for each other in our sorrow and suffering.

And this loving, helping, forgiving and healing each other is now possible precisely because the kingdom is already here among us. This is a very important insight. Our loving each other is not a precondition for the kingdom. Rather, it is a sign that the kingdom is here. God is not standing outside our world, saying, 'When you begin to love each other I will come among you.' He is saying, 'I am among you, offering you the power to love as I love.' At the Last Supper Jesus prays that we may be one in love, 'so that the world may believe it was you who sent me' (John 17:21). The world will know that the kingdom is here when it sees us going out to each other in love. Our love for one another is not a precondition of the kingdom but a sign that it is here. But while the kingdom is among us, it is always still coming because we are weak and we need God and his power daily. So Jesus tells us to pray to the Father that the kingdom will come in its fullness.

The kingdom is present when you see people doing more than you would expect, when you see the courage and serenity of someone battling with cancer or AIDS, when you hear of someone forgiving an enemy who treated them with great cruelty, when you see a wife's heroic patience with an alcoholic husband, when you see parent's tender love for a handicapped child, when someone breaks a drug habit, when a social worker battles against great odds to bring dignity to exploited people. This is the kingdom among us. Ordinary people can do more than we expect, because they are no longer ordinary people when they open themselves to the power of the kingdom, when they realise they are not alone, not depending on mere human resources. They hear and trust the word of Jesus: 'My Father goes on working and so do I.'

Jesus invites us to seek the kingdom, to enter it now. He asks us to make it our priority, to put it before all else because it is precisely there that we shall find the hope and power and courage to cope with everything else. He says the Father knows all our needs and cares. 'Set your hearts on his kingdom first, and on his righteousness, and all these other things will be given you as well' (Matthew 6:33). Jesus is really asking us not to try to cope alone, since now we are never alone any more. To enter this kingdom and experience its power we must become as children. We must have the trust of children if we are to claim the promises of Jesus. At baptism, when we chose this Jesus, we rejected the 'empty promises' of Satan. The evil one is full of promises, but, coming from the father of lies, they are empty. He cannot deliver. The Lord we chose in faith also makes promises. If we trust him, we shall discover with the Psalmist that Yahweh is 'always true to his promises' (Psalm 145:13). The kingdom of God is God among us, hard at work fulfilling those promises.

15

SLEEPING BEAUTY

'I tell you solemnly, anyone who does not welcome the kingdom of God like a little child will never enter it' (Mark 10:15). When Jesus invites us to become as children that we may experience the fruits of the kingdom, he is inviting us to share in an experience that had become a reality for him, the reality on which he based his message, his whole life, indeed, and eventually his death. That reality was his own personal experience of God as Abba, his own conviction that he was the beloved child of his Father, God. Jesus was the first Jew to use this word, 'Abba', when addressing Yahweh. The word suggests a very special relationship of love, intimacy and trust. Abba was the word used by a very young Jewish child calling to its father. It is close to our words, dada, daddy, papa. It is full of affection and total trust.

When we say Jesus was a true man, like us in all our limitations except sin, we are saying Jesus had to grow, not only physically and intellectually, but spiritually and emotionally. St Luke speaks of this. 'Jesus increased in wisdom, in stature, and in favour with God and men' (Luke 2:52). Sometimes we might wonder what Jesus did during the long thirty years of his hidden life. Luke says simply that 'he grew'. Jesus grew in his relationship with people and God. Mary and Joseph would have introduced the child to Yahweh and taught him his prayers. We can imagine how those parents would have been so glad to share with their son their own love and deep trust in Yahweh. Prayer must have been the great meeting-place with his Father. There, over the years, Jesus grows in intimacy with God his Father. He grows in understanding of the Father's love, experiencing in his depths that he is the beloved Son, discovering his hidden self. It grows on him over the years as a young prince, born the son of the King, his father, gradually becomes aware of who he is and what he is called to do.

During all these years Jesus is a disciple learning from his Father, God. Notice the way Jesus uses the word 'Amen' in his teaching. We use this little word a lot in our prayers. It is a rich word. It says yes to what we have just heard. Jesus uses it differently. He puts it not at the end of a statement, but at the beginning. 'Amen, amen, I say to you . . .'. In this way he tells us that what he says to us is what he has heard from his Father. His Amen is to the Father's word which he has heard and now shares with us. 'What the Father has told me is what I speak' (John 12:50). And again he says, 'The Son can do nothing by himself; he can only do what he sees the Father doing' (John 5:19). This must refer to his prayer experience. If Jesus is able to describe the father of the prodigal son running down the road to embrace his boy, it is because he has 'seen' this happen in his prayer. In his heart Jesus is convinced not only that he is the beloved Son, but that all of us are loved unconditionally by this Father. That's what gave him the power to work miracles of compassion and heal the broken hearts of sinners and of the rejects of society. This was the source of the power of his words. He spoke the truth and, when people heard it, there was an echo within them.

Now when he invites us to become as children so that we can enter the kingdom, he is not primarily thinking of heaven after death and suggesting that we become sinless to qualify for entrance. I think he is speaking of the kingdom we have been reflecting on, the loving, active, healing power of God among us. Unless we become like Jesus, the first child of Abba, we shall not experience the blessing of this kingdom. We must have Jesus' conviction of God's real presence in his world, a presence of love that is dynamic and wants to do infinitely more than we can ask or even imagine. We have to become full of the child's joyful wonder and trust. Someone has said that what we need is not more wonders, but more wonder. Our world, our existence is full of wonder if only we could see with the eyes of a child.

As children we believed in fairy stories and moved at ease in a land of wonder and mystery, a land where we held conversations with trees and animals and inanimate objects. It was a land where anything could happen, where dragons were slain, where ugly toads became charming princes, where Sleeping Beauty awoke to life, where dusty, cobwebbed chests opened to reveal glittering treasure, where haunting ghosts were chased away or turned out to be friends in disguise, where old dungeon doors were opened and prisoners were set free, where young lovers were reunited. As children we moved unself-consciously in this world of wonder.

Then, years passed and we grew up and became wise, as we thought, worldly wise. We may have smiled at our childish fancies as we entered what we believed to be reality. In some ways it was like leaving a garden to enter a desert. In this 'real' world it seemed difficult to find an oasis of true joy, pure love, innocent peace. It looked more like a wasteland of harsh experience, of a new kind of pretending, of deception, of hollow joy, betrayed trust, broken dreams.

But then, as more years pass by and we adapt to the world as we meet it, it is to be hoped that our picture of what constitutes reality will broaden and soften, will brighten and deepen, so that, with the passing of the years, we may grow even wiser still. We grow and learn through suffering patiently borne, through the experience of real love and friendship, through renewed joy in the annual miracle of the first spring flowers, through just hanging in despite heavy troubles, through patience with the ambiguities of life, finding deeper meaning in the mystery. We grow into deeper wisdom and begin to believe again in wonder and in mystery, in the certainty that we are made for joy, not sorrow, for love, not hatred. We begin to realise deep down that, as children, we were in touch with the true reality. Witches and dragons will not have the last word; our mourning will be turned to dancing, our sorrow to joy; tears will be wiped away. Love is the ultimate reality, the only absolute, the great imperative. The one who assures us of all this is the Son of Abba, the Eternal Child. He staked his very life on this and Abba said Amen in the resurrection.

When I was a child I enjoyed the feast of Christmas. I did not think too much about it. I just enjoyed it. When I grew up and was trying to understand what religion and faith were all about, I considered Christmas the great feast for children with its fairy-tale atmosphere. Then years later I began to think I was wrong and that surely Christmas was an adult's feast. Only an adult could appreciate the great reality that lay behind God's incredible love in becoming one of us which gave all the meaning to Christmas. Now I have moved again and am certain that only the adult who has become a child again can thoroughly enjoy Christmas and celebrate it properly. Our deepest instincts, which believe in fairy stories and happy endings, are correct.

Someone says there is a great sign over the gate of heaven which reads 'Children Only'. And if that worries you, I am told there is another notice on the gate which reads. 'Adults will be admitted if accompanied by Children'. Jesus did say the gate into eternal life is small. Certainly the entrance to the kingdom here on earth is small and narrow. Only a child will fit in. But will the gate be open? It's a mysterious gate. It opens when it sees a child! And a child has no problem with that wonder. It is the adult who wants to have control, to make sure he has the key. The child will trust. The kingdom is gift. We cannot control it. If you try to control it, you immunise yourself against it. Accept it like a child. Each of us is invited in. We can be transformed. Sleeping Beauty can be awakened in each of us.

16

CLIMBING THE LADDER

In his teaching about life and about the kingdom, Jesus often uses the image of a seed. It is a simple but very enlightening image. A seed must grow and growth takes time. This involves waiting and waiting calls for patience. Life is a mystery and in its own way so is growth. 'This is what the kingdom of God is like. A man throws seed on the land. Night and day, while he sleeps, when he is awake, the seed is sprouting and growing; how, he does not know' (Mark 4:26-28). Growth shares in the mystery of life itself. Paul writes to the Corinthians, 'I did the planting, Apollos did the watering, but God made things grow. Neither the planter nor the waterer matters: only God, who makes things grow' (1 Corinthians 3:6-7). Life is a mysterious growth process and God is intimately involved. There is no instant fruit, no instant flower. There is no instant completion of life, no instant fullness of life whether physical, emotional or spiritual. A further dimension of mystery suggested by the image of the seed is that the future fullness and beauty of flower or fruit are potentially present in the seed. As this potential is fulfilled we say the seed 'grows'. As we noted earlier, we do not say the seed 'changes'. The word 'change' suggests becoming something else, something different. The word 'grow' suggests the realisation of what is already present. When Paul prays that our 'hidden self may grow strong', he is praying that we become more and more our own true selves. And he assures us that God is actively at work in that growth.

We saw that Jesus himself grew in favour with God and people. In certain obvious ways we all grow in age, knowledge, skills etc. as life goes on. It is to be hoped that our physical, intellectual and emotional growth will be paralleled by our spiritual growth. But this area of our spiritual growth proves to be a problem area and one that can cause a lot of discouragement. We believe that this is the most important area of our lives. Yet, the experience of many people is that it is the area where we observe the least progress. Most of us are disappointed with ourselves. We feel that we have made little progress and, despite years of trying to live the Christian life, we are not much better than when we started. Indeed, some would say they are worse now than they were years ago. Not only do many of our old faults stay with us and we feel it is the same old me, but worse, the ongoing years reveal dark and ugly possibilities of evil in me not suspected in earlier years.

I believe the picture is not nearly as bleak as people imagine and that our negative views of our spiritual state would not be shared by God. I think the reason why many people judge themselves harshly is that they limit their judgment to externals; they think of growth chiefly as moral progress. They have false and unreal expectations of what spiritual growth is all about. People with such false ideals can be quite upset, even shocked, when they hear Scripture say, 'Be perfect like your heavenly Father.' After years of Christian life they feel they are light years away from such an ideal. I wish to offer some thoughts which help me in this matter and which may help you. We will always experience some inner tension in this area. Not only that, but I believe that such tension is a good sign. The worst symptom of a sick spiritual life is self-satisfaction.

The desire to see results and notice progress in our Christian life and spiritual growth is very natural. We all like to feel we are doing well in whatever work or project we have undertaken. We like to succeed. It encourages us. But in the area of the spiritual life this is a tricky, even danger-ous exercise. It is natural to want to see progress, but maybe it is too natural! It could ignore the deep truth that growth in the spiritual life is not like growth in business or sporting skills or in mastering a language. The spiritual life is lived out in a faith context where the last can turn out to be the first.The spiritual life tends to defy analysis and measurement. We cannot plot it on a graph and admire the upward curve.

The only people in the gospel who felt sure of their spiritual growth were the Pharisees. For them the line on the graph rose steadily all the time. And today we meet religious people who feel quite sure that their salvation is already achieved. True holiness, real spiritual growth, is the most unself-conscious phenomenon. When Mary was told she had found favour with God, we are told that 'she was deeply disturbed by these words' (Luke 1:29). If Simon the Pharisee were told that he had found favour with God, he would have said to the angel, 'Tell me something I don't know.' And that's precisely why poor Simon would not have an angelic visitor to tell him he had found favour with God.

Spiritual growth is not synonymous with moral perfection. Many people think their growth in Christian life is to be measured by the degree of control they achieve over moral weakness and failure. This is not so. True holiness and growth are compatible with moral failure. Nor should growth in the spiritual life be identified with an intellectual grasp of the doctrines of the Church. After Vatican II many, including priests and religious, were thrown into turmoil by the changes, by new teaching, by the abandoning of old, safe positions, by accepting that there is truth in other faiths, even in non-faith people. Again, it must be stressed that it is possible to grow in holiness while being beset by doubts, ambiguities and uncertainties.

I suggest an image which may offset some of our discouragement. When we think of growth and progress, we usually think of it as an outward and upward movement. This is behind the graph idea. We think of ourselves climbing to some point of perfection outside of us and away above us. The image of a ladder comes to mind. We see ourselves go up a few rungs as we feel we are making some progress. But then we crash. We slip back down the ladder. We feel we are back where we started or even on a lower rung. Now I suggest we think of the goal of perfection or growth not as outside and above us but as within, deep down at the centre of our being. Our faith journey is not climbing up into the clouds but a journey into the deep, into the heart of reality, into the depths of the mystery of God within us.

The motion now is not so much upwards as circular, covering old familiar ground, passing familiar landmarks on the way but, it is to be hoped, over the years, penetrating more deeply the mystery, the reality lying beneath all the external signs. We journey through the familiar seasons of the Church calendar, Advent, Christmas, Lent, Easter and Pentecost, and each year we discover more meaning and riches in these holy days and seasons. We read familiar Scripture passages and prayers and discover new and hidden treasure we had not noticed before. We are present at baptisms, weddings, funerals and slowly again over the years are touched by an awareness of something far greater and more wonderful than ourselves. We receive familiar sacraments and now are motivated by personal desire rather than a sense of duty to Church law. And when we find ourselves in the terrible no-go area of suffering and tragedy, it is to be hoped that there may be less anger and bitterness and some kind of awareness that this pain is not wasted as we deepen in appreciation of the suffering of Christ.

The model for our spiritual growth is not a state of moral perfection. The elder boy in the parable of the Prodigal Son seemed to have reached such a state. He never broke a single law and worked diligently on his father's farm. But he had no love for his father or his young brother. At the end of the story he is all alone, sulking in the yard, while the others are celebrating inside. Here we have a frightening lesson, that it is possible to keep all God's laws and still have no love of God in our hearts. The real key to spiritual growth is love and the model of that love is Christ. The gospel image for the growth to which we are called is Christ himself. St Paul invites us to put on Christ, to have the mind of Christ, to become other Christs. Each of us, in our own limited but unique way, must try to love like Christ, must try to reflect his compassion, his understanding, his forgiveness. We are called to be Christ-like, each in our own special way. That is why it is so important that we accept our own self, our own unique self.

Since there is only one you, this means that you can reveal Christ in a way that no one else can. Gerard Manley Hopkins reflects on this. He speaks of the unique creation, not only of each person, but of each creature. Each creature, he says, does its own special thing for which it was created and makes its own unique contribution to the great symphony of the universe. But the vocation of each person is more wonderful and mysterious. Each person, in living out his or her own true and deepest self, reveals some feature of Christ's image. Each person, he says:

> Acts in God's eye what in God's eye he is –
> Christ – for Christ plays in ten thousand places,
> Lovely in limbs, and lovely in eyes not his
> To the Father through the features of men's faces.

17

FRIENDSHIP WITH THE LORD

We have been speaking about progress in the spiritual life, of growth in the Christian life. Let us move beyond these expressions and consider the same reality under a different light. In a sense there is no such thing as Christianity or the Christian life. There is Christ and people who meet him, know him and relate to him. Christians are people who have come to know Christ. They have been inspired by his love and try to respond with love. At the heart of our faith is a person, not a creed, not a moral code but a person. Creed, dogma, moral code – all have their place in religion, but not the first place, not the centre. They are neither the source of nor the inspiration for the life we call Christian.

It all began when people met and were attracted by a man called Jesus. They became his disciples and followed him. They were sure he was to usher in a new and golden age. Then they were traumatised by his sudden collapse, his arrest, crucifixion and death, which destroyed all their dreams. But then they were totally transformed by meeting him again, risen from the dead, alive and among them in forgiveness, compassion, love and power. They were driven by their experience to share this good news with others. They were sharing a living person, a loving friend with power to heal their hurts and give deep meaning to life. They were not preaching an ideology or looking for members for a new religion. This was the experience of those first followers who had known Jesus in the flesh.

The first generation of believers, who listened to those friends of the Lord and who themselves had not met Jesus in the flesh, were equally certain through the gift of the Holy Spirit that this Jesus truly was alive and with them and for them and was worthy of their love, a love which filled them with joy and was so real that they were ready to give up their lives for him. St Peter rejoices in the faith of these believers. 'You did not see Jesus, yet you love him; and still without seeing him, you are filled with a joy so glorious that it cannot be described, because you believe' (1 Peter 1:8-9). We live in the time of the Lord. He is risen and present to us as he was to that first generation. The same gift of faith is offered to us. The same gift of God's Holy Spirit is poured out upon us so that we can know him, not just know about him, but know him and, knowing him, come to love him and be filled with joy because of that love.

If we were to look at our Christian life from this point of view, it could become a warmer, life-giving reality. The Lord reveals himself to me in faith and asks for my friendship. As life goes on, do I feel I am getting to know him better through my experience of prayer, through reading and meditating on his living word in scripture, through meeting him in sacraments and people? Some Christians might not describe their spiritual life in that way, but I believe this is the experience of many. There is a sense of friendship with the Lord. Maybe we should draw attention to it more often and encourage each other. For many, it has found expression in what we call devotion to the Sacred Heart. I think it is revealed in many common expressions, as when we say to each other, 'The Lord won't let you down.' 'He understands.' 'He put up with a lot himself.' 'He won't be outdone in generosity.' Such expressions suggest a warm, personal friendship.

It is a pity our religion has not been presented in a more personal fashion, that the person of the Lord Jesus has not been placed more clearly at the centre. One reason for this may be related to what we said earlier about the way we come to know Jesus. Most of us first met Jesus as God, to be adored and worshipped. We neglected the other side of the mystery, equally a matter of faith, that he is a true human person like us, one who calls us friends and seeks our friendship. The words spoken to Peter at the lakeside after the resurrection are also addressed to you and me.

'Do you love me?' (John 21:15). It does not mean that if we say yes and choose Jesus we will immediately understand everything about him and will follow him perfectly. No. This is the work of a lifetime. But it could mean a new joy and warmth in our faith.

We can learn much and also be greatly encouraged by the story of St Peter's own relationship with Jesus. It began when Peter realised that this wonderful person, Jesus, chose him and wanted his friendship and help even when he knew, on Peter's own admission, that Peter was a sinful man. This peak experience in Peter's life occurred one morning in his boat on the lake after a miraculous catch of fish. This miracle told Peter that he was in the presence of someone very special and holy. Peter, immediately aware of his own sinfulness, cried out, 'Leave me, Lord; I am a sinful man' (Luke 5:8). Instead of leaving him, the Lord drew closer and told Peter he wanted to have him as his companion and workmate. Peter's life would never be the same again after this experience. It was a moment of deep conversion, a moment of true healing of the whole person, when Peter realised that he was totally accepted just as he was. He realised that his weak and sinful state was known and embraced by a love and holiness utterly transcending himself.

As time passed, Peter grew in understanding this Lord and friend. When Jesus asked one day, 'Who do you say that I am?', Peter answered, 'You are the Christ' (Matthew 16:16). But the next moment Peter showed he had much to learn. Jesus spoke of the suffering he would have to endure and Peter immediately protested, 'This must not happen to you' (Matthew 16:22). I am sure Peter did not want his friend Jesus to suffer. But I suspect other motives at work. Following Christ should mean glory, not suffering. But the suffering did come and when it did, Peter was terribly confused. In the garden of Gesthsemane he pulled the sword to defend his friend, but was told to put it away. Jesus was dragged off into the night. We are told, 'Peter followed him at a distance' (Matthew 26:58). This says a lot about Peter and about ourselves. Peter followed Jesus, but 'at a distance'. He followed Jesus because he was his friend and he loved him, but he followed 'at a distance' because he was afraid. Is it not a picture of many of Christ's friends and followers, a picture of ourselves? We too often follow at a distance, but our friend Jesus can cope with this weakness.

When Jesus was being tried and tortured, Peter was outside in the courtyard warming himself by a charcoal fire. A servant girl accused him of being a follower of Jesus. Peter answered, 'I do not know the man' (Matthew 26:72). Peter said more than he realised. There was a great irony here. Peter shouted out a lie to protect himself. But was it a lie? Was it not in a deep way the truth? Peter did not yet know his friend. He did not understand what was going on. He did not yet understand the place of suffering in the service of love. He couldn't understand this kind of love, the genuine thing being lived out by Jesus. Peter did not know the man Jesus who is the love of God made visible. Neither do we know how good our friend Jesus is and how privileged we are that he calls us friend. But Peter was learning all the time and, in that scene by the lakeside, he would answer his friend's question, 'Peter, do you love me?' with that wonderful prayer, 'Lord, you know everything; you know I love you' (John 21:17).

Can this be our prayer, our word from the heart to our Lord and friend? We have spoken of the discouragement we feel in our lack of progress in the spiritual life. But when we look at it now in terms of personal friendship with Jesus, hopefully we too can make our own, Peter's prayer, 'Lord, you know everything, you know all my lukewarmness, my fears, my failure to understand your ways, how I have so often let you down out of fear and selfishness, how I try to avoid sacrifice at all cost. Yet Lord, deep, deep down you know that I love you.' Jesus our friend understands. It was he who used the image of the seed to tell us that growth takes time. There is no instant growth, no instant holiness. The seed needs time to grow. Friendship takes time. Love needs time. This is a deep truth which in our world has become obscure. Jack Dominian, who writes with such understanding of love and marriage today, says, 'Love cannot be found in the transient, superficial, shallow.' Jesus notes that the seed that falls in shallow soil springs up quickly, but dies equally quickly. Dominian says that the evil of our day is not so much the trivialisation of sex but the trivialisation of persons and personal relationships. People want quick, easy encounters with equally quick disengagement when troubles come. But true love should endure all and is tested by time. The growth of our personal friendship with the Lord may be slow because of our weakness, but surely it must be the source of our deepest joy in life. Again we remember Peter's words to the first Christians. 'You did not see him, yet you love him; and still without seeing him, you are already filled with a joy so glorious that it cannot be described' (1 Peter 1:8-9). This friendship will continue to grow until we die and beyond, as we explore the infinite mystery of love. Let us see our faith life as a love story and not a chasing after perfection in the Christian life. We are baptised into Christ, not into Christianity. Before the world was formed, we were chosen in Jesus Christ to live through love in his presence (Ephesians 1:4). Let us be in love, not with the spiritual life, but with the Lord.

18

MAY GOD UNCOVER HIS FACE TO YOU

The discouragement which many people experience when trying to evaluate their progress and growth in the spiritual life comes from the persistent evidence of our failure and human weakness, our broken resolutions, the tenacity of old faults and even the revelation of new, unsuspected evil. We said that we must see our spiritual life as a faith experience not subject to the same rules of analysis and evaluation which apply when assessing progress in other pursuits. We also said it is misleading to objectify the spiritual life. We are not pursuing an ideal called the spiritual life. We cannot be in love with the spiritual life. In a sense there is no such reality. There is Jesus Christ, true God and true man, offering me his love and inviting my love in response. Here we enter a land of wonder and mystery.

The mentality of our modern consumer society is alien to the sense of mystery. I believe the consumer mentality affects us more than we realise by leading us subconsciously to see our spiritual life as some kind of religious commodity. Our society offers many different commodities for our pleasure, our convenience and our fulfilment. Manufacturers and advertisers make claims for their products and guarantee they will satisfy, or else we can have our money back. We are invited to evaluate these goods, objects and commodities by a measurable criterion of satisfaction. Do they deliver what they promise? Without noticing it we can objectify religious practices such as prayer, the Mass, devotions and sacraments, and try to evaluate them by the same criteria we apply to the goods offered by the supermarkets. We can find ourselves saying, 'Mass does little for me', or 'I try to give time to prayer but it is so dry and fruitless.' The conclusion in such instances may be, 'Let me try something else', which may deliver the spiritual goods!

In our faith world we must stress wonder and mystery. We deal with the infinite, transcendent God seeking us in love. We must be prepared to allow ourselves to be possessed by this mystery rather than trying to be in control, aiming at achieving certain specific results. St Paul says we are the temple of God. Maybe we are overconcerned with the building, with the externals, the scaffolding, as it were, our religious duties and practices. All of these are important and helpful but maybe we should move inside the building, to the holy place, to the sanctuary where God dwells in our innermost being.

I may ask, if I see my spiritual life as building a personal relationship with God revealed in Jesus my friend, rather than a striving to achieve a spiritual ideal, will the same sense of discouragement not assail me? Thus, instead of measuring up to an ideal I let down my friend. I suggest not. When I see my spiritual life as a relationship with a loving friend there are some new, important differences. It is true that now, when I fail, I feel I have disappointed a friend, but who is this friend? He is so special. He is known to me as totally understanding, compassionate, steadfast. There is nothing petty or mean about him. He knows my human heart from the inside, but he is also greater than my heart and is infinitely patient. He accepts me as I am and gradually his constant love will heal my weakness and lead me into love.

Another big difference is that in friendship two people are involved. You cannot fall in love with an ideology or an ideal. Deep down I feel the call of Jesus, my friend, and try to respond, despite repeated failure. But he is very much involved and wants the friendship to succeed. While I, in my limited way, am seeking him, he is also seeking me. God wants not only to reveal himself to me, but to give himself to me. Inspired scripture is the guarantee of this. It tells the story of God seeking us, seeking me. The message spoken for centuries through the prophets and spoken now in our day through the Son is so simple and yet such a mystery. The message is, 'I love you.' In the prophet Isaiah we are called 'the sought-after' (Isaiah 62:11). Here is the source of our confidence as we enter into that journey which takes the whole of our lifetime, the journey into God. Our confidence is not based on our determination or will-power, but on the mystery that God wants this friendship more than we do. St Augustine realised this when he prayed, 'You have made us for yourself, O Lord, and our hearts are restless till they rest in you.' And a modern writer on prayer, Carlo Carretto, writes, 'My seeking him would have been in vain if, before all time, he had not sought me.'

Here is a blessing prayer taken from the Old Testament:

> May Yahweh bless you and keep you.
> May Yahweh let his face shine on you and be
>   gracious to you.
> May Yahweh uncover his face to you and bring
>   you peace.
> *Numbers 6:24-26*

Now let us notice the verses that introduce this blessing prayer, 'Yaweh spoke to Moses and said, "Say this to Aaron and his sons: This is how you are to bless the sons of Israel. You shall say to them: May Yahweh etc..." ' (Numbers 6:22-23). So here we have a blessing prayer composed not by Moses or Aaron, but by God himself. He says to us, 'When you bless each other, say these words.' This means these are the very blessings God wants us to have. God lets us see inside his own heart and tells us in this way that he wants to uncover his face to us. Jesus continues this blessing work of his Father. At the Last Supper he speaks to this same God and says, 'Father, I have made your name known to them and will continue to make it known' (John 17:26). And, for the Jew, the name was not just a label but stood for the inner being of the person. Here again is the kingdom, God amongst us wanting to share his inner being with us.

One gateway into this kingdom, one place where we meet this God and share his life, is prayer. I was going to entitle this chapter 'Prayer' but decided against it. In fact what we have been talking about all the time is prayer. This friendship with the Lord is prayer. Some of our difficulties in prayer arise out of a wrong approach or misleading attitudes to prayer. Often, when we speak of prayer, we think of it as a Christian duty, one among many, which we must perform if we are to grow in the Christian life. There is a suggestion that it is something we must do to please God, the omission of which would displease him. There is a further hint that God will love me more if I pray. Such attitudes give a very false idea of the reality of prayer and can rob me of the rich nourishment, the life that awaits me, if I take prayer seriously.

Why should I pray? Not in order to make God love me, but because I am sure he loves me. What is more natural than to want to be with the one who loves me, to speak to a loved one, to listen or just to be with a lover. We pray not to make something happen, but because something incredible is happening all the time. God is seeking me to share his caring love and power. I need time to stop, become aware and savour this mystery. We pray not that we may attract God's attention but because we are certain that we are the centre of his attention for each moment of each day. God is the singer, I am his song. We need prayer to become aware of this and to say 'Amen' to his constant recreating activity in our lives.

Prayer is not a duty. Prayer is life itself. Prayer is being with this God who nourishes us with his love. Prayer is being the branch drawing life and nourishment from the vine. Prayer is being with my lover. Let us ask a silly question. It can help us. The question is: 'Who invented prayer? Was it the Church or some saint or guru?' Do you see why the question is silly? It is like asking who invented holding hands and embracing! These are things you do when you are in love. Prayer is what you do when you are in love.

101

Prayer is not an escape from reality in search of consolation to make life bearable. Prayer is the exploration of that deepest reality in which we live and move and have our being and which is the source of all joy and consolation and power, namely that we are unconditionally loved each moment by our God who rejoices in us and wants to renew us by his love.

> Yahweh your God is in your midst,
> a victorious warrior.
> He will exult with joy over you,
> He will renew you by his love;
> he will dance with shouts of joy for you
> as on a day of festival.
> *Zephaniah 3:17*

19

PRAYER – THE HIDDEN LIFE

Recent years have seen a great new interest in prayer and a great awakening of desire for some experience of prayer life. There is an abundance of books and tapes (audio and visual) describing the prayer methods and techniques used in different religious cultures. People flock to gurus and spiritual guides for help. This interest in prayer may be partly a reaction to the materialism of our age. But it must also be evidence of the human heart's hunger for God and the activity of the Holy Spirit who is given to us to help us with our prayer. We surely must rejoice at this sincere and widespread interest in prayer. At the same time, I believe there could be some subtle and misleading side-effects of the very publicity that accompanies this welcome interest. I suggest two possible side-effects and hope that by noticing and considering them, we may deepen our appreciation of the true nature of prayer.

One of these possible misleading side-effects could be that we might be led to see prayer as a skill, a technique, something we can learn and master if we read the right book or sit at the feet of some well-known guru. This again could be the subtle influence of our consumer society. Prayer may appear to be marketed like some commodity or appliance. You can learn this technique and develop a facility for prayer and it will bring certain desired blessings. This attitude would destroy the mystery of our faith, the mystery of God and of the unique relationship between God and each person. It could tend towards magic rather than true religion. Prayer is not a technique by which we can control or manipulate God and achieve certain results. We come to prayer with awe and wonder and a great sense of privilege as we humbly seek the face of the transcendent God. And we come with confidence, not because of any skill we have developed but because this God wants to uncover his face to us.

A second possible dangerous side-effect of this widespread publicity about prayer is that it might lead some to feel inadequate and discouraged. People could begin to feel that, if they have not read the latest book or listened to the latest tape or attended a prayer seminar, they could not have a deep experience of prayer. These books, tapes and seminars all cost money. One person said to me a while ago, 'It's becoming very expensive now to have a personal relationship with the Lord!' There was no admission fee to the Sermon on the Mount and no hand-outs after it. But it's not the question of cost which concerns me here, but the more subtle problem that people could be discouraged if they thought that progress in prayer depended on the many prayer-aids that are available. Now it is good and right that we should read the literature on prayer and learn from reliable teachers, both old and new, but we must also be sure that prayer is a gift which should be sought with humility. And we must repeat that our confidence in prayer is based, not on special skills, but on God's call to our hearts, on his desire for our love and on our sincere desire to return that love and surrender our lives to him.

Let us ask what kind of people Jesus was talking to when he said, 'If anyone loves me he will keep my word, and my Father will love him, and we shall come to him and make our home with him' (John 14:23), or again, 'I am the vine, you are the branches. Whoever remains in me, with me in him, bears fruit in plenty' (John 15:5) or again, 'I have made your name known to them, so that the love with which you loved me may be in them' (John 17:26). Jesus himself tells us that it was to the poor and simple, and even sinners, that he was sent to reveal this great mystery of the Father's love and his wish to dwell in the hearts of his people. 'It was then that, filled with joy by the Holy Spirit, he said, "I bless you, Father, Lord of heaven and earth, for hiding these things from the learned and the clever and revealing them to mere children" ' (Luke 10:21).

Someone has said that the only equipment we need for

prayer is time. But, above all, there must be desire for the Lord and his friendship. It is easy to say the prayer of the Psalmist with our lips. 'As a doe longs for running streams, so longs my soul for you, my God' (Psalm 42:1). But to be so serious about it that I will discipline myself and make time – that is another matter. It is easier to spend an hour reading a book about prayer than to spend the hour praying. I like the cartoon which shows two great gateways. Over one is written 'Heaven' and thousands of joyful, simple people are pouring through the gate. Over the other is written 'Lectures on Heaven' and through this gate streams a large flow of rather serious-looking intellectuals, theologians and religious! We need to become children to enter the kingdom of prayer. But that does not mean that prayer is child's play. It is helpful here to be honest and admit that, in a sense, prayer is not easy. It is no offence to God to say that prayer is difficult. If we are honest and accept this, we might investigate why it is difficult and be prepared, in spite of difficulties, to persevere in seeking the Lord's face in prayer.

Many give up prayer through disappointment, which mostly stems from false expectations of prayer. Many hope they will arrive after some time at distraction-free prayer which will bring feelings of consolation. Or they hope for an obvious improvement in their moral and spiritual life. When these good results do not seem to be forthcoming and when prayer, after years of perseverance, remains dry and distracted, they feel it is a waste of time. Even worse, some feel ashamed and think that their poor prayer is almost an offence to God.

Surely, they think, if one sincerely seeks God and places oneself in the presence of the loving God, it should not happen that within minutes our minds can leave that presence and be distracted by the most trivial concerns, even by impure desires, while only the poor body remains at the place of prayer! Surely this cannot be pleasing to God or bring him glory. So they conclude that this kind of exercise is a waste of time quite unworthy of God. Surely it would be better to give this time to something worthwhile for God, like some charitable work for my neighbour.

This is false reasoning. We cannot and must not judge prayer in this way. Prayer is not meant to produce results like that. A deep prayer life is perfectly compatible with much dryness and distraction. Measurable, growing control over our human weakness is not the criterion of our prayer. We do not pray to achieve results. Prayer is more about receiving than achieving. To receive you have to be there. We are not praying to develop our inner selves or achieve some kind of self-fulfilment. In prayer we forget about self; we empty self and open ourselves to God's activity, which is infinitely more important than our activity. Prayer is its own end, to be with the Lord. If we persevere and are faithful, God will keep his promises and reveal himself. 'When you seek me you shall find me, when you seek me with all your heart; I will let you find me. It is Yahweh who speaks' (Jeremiah 29:13-14). This seeking and finding is the work of our lifetime.

It is a slow process and, paradoxically, can be painful. In a sense this must be so. It would be naive to expect that, as we enter more deeply into the mystery of God, we would see and understand him more clearly with a clarity which would enable us to describe him to others. It is the transcendent God of infinite majesty, wonder and mystery that we seek. It is the ultimate reality that we explore. Some people accuse those who pray of choosing an easy option, of escaping from the reality of injustice and suffering into a world of forgetting and consolation. Surely this would be a very shallow idea of reality and prayer. Is reality to be identified with injustice and suffering? To wait on God in prayer, in a cloud of unknowing, can hardly be described as consolation. It can be totally humbling, even devastating, challenging faith at its deepest level; is there anybody there? Some years ago, in a film entitled *The Ruling Class*, Peter O'Toole played the part of an eccentric nobleman who felt sure he was God. When asked why he thought this, he replied: 'Well, you see, they say that to pray is to talk to God. Now, whenever I pray, I find that I am talking to myself!' Many believers who try to pray would admit, if they were honest, that this eccentric nobleman was not the only one to have this thought.

Prayer calls for faith, love, humility. How humbling to enter the presence of the Lord and some minutes later find yourself engaged in some trivial, even base exercise of the imagination. Would it not be better to be out working for the good of my neighbour? The question is, is there a personal God who listens and speaks and wants my love? Or, is there only my neighbour, and is loving him or her enough? What would Jesus say? He speaks of loving God with the whole heart and says that is the first commandment. I must resist the temptation to think my prayer is a waste of time. If I persevere, I can come to believe that, although nothing seems to happen, the moments of stillness, when I seek awareness of the Lord, are the most important and precious moments of my day, no matter what else I may do that day.

Jesus came to save the world. As it turned out, he lived only thirty-three years on earth. Thirty of those years were spent in the obscurity of Nazareth. Doing what? We could say 'nothing', or we could say 'growing'. Our sense of urgency and efficiency are offended by this strange choice of his, this extraordinary disproportion, thirty years a-growing and only three years of active evangelisation, and so much to be done. Judged by our standards of efficiency, Jesus wasted many years, but, again and again, he is inviting us to find and live by his values and standards, to think and live by the thoughts of God, not humankind. During those hidden years Jesus was often with his Father in prayer. I doubt if he was looking for 'results'. His compassion, his love, his trust, his mercy, his courage and his death were the essential fruit of those years of hidden growth. Our prayer may often seem poor and wasted. Let us see it through God's eyes. Our prayer is our hidden life. It is humble and hidden, but it is life.

20

PRAYER AND MYSTERY

Prayer is surrender to God. It is letting God be God. It is accepting my creaturehood. It is humble exploration of the mystery. Prayer breaks through the barrier of familiarity. We are used to the word 'God'. We say the word and think we know the reality it stands for. But we cannot know God as we might know some object or creature. God is not just one other creature of the universe. God is not *another*, nor even *the* other, he is simply Other. God is the origin, ground and source of all being. This concept is difficult for us. It is so difficult that we try to cope by making God small and manageable. This has always been a temptation for us, to make God in our own image and likeness. Why did God forbid the making of idols? Did he fear competition? No. Maybe it was because if we make images, we can begin to imagine that we know what God is like. This might not seem to be such a great danger in these more sophisticated times. We are not likely to make images of wood or stone. But there is a more subtle danger, that of making conceptual idols, of trying to tie God down to a definition, to a dogma. Jesus came to reveal the true God. He came to set us free from idolatry and fear. But also we can say he came to set God free. He came to set God free from our narrow human definitions. The hardest word Jesus spoke to the Pharisees was to accuse them of not knowing God. They were the official religious teachers, but Jesus said to them, 'My glory is conferred by the Father, by the one of whom you say, "He is our God", although you do not know him' (John 8:54-55).

When we speak of our faith as growing in a personal relationship with God, we are not thinking of growing in understanding him more clearly. It would be childish to expect this. We should rather expect the opposite, that we will become more and more aware of how little we know.

The sense of wonder and mystery should grow. We should find ourselves agreeing with the saints who said, 'What we know about God is more untrue than true.' We will begin to understand how St Thomas Aquinas, one of the most brilliant theologians, at the end of his days, could dismiss all his brilliant writings as 'mere straw'.

In the Old Testament the great sign of God's presence was the Cloud. When the Cloud descended and filled the Tent of the Tabernacle, all prostrated in worship, knowing God was present. In later times the mystics used the Cloud as an image of our inability to understand God. It suggested darkness and absence of understanding. This is paradox. The Cloud is simultaneously the image for the Presence and the Absence. Again the mystics say, 'He who says, does not know; he who knows, does not say.' We have to go beyond words, concepts and definitions. The author of *The Cloud of Unknowing* speaks of a different kind of 'knowing', namely by loving. 'By love he may be touched and embraced, by thought never.' St John says, 'Anyone who fails to love can never have known God' (1 John 4:8).

Is all this talk of God's otherness not frightening and discouraging for someone who wants to pray? If we reflect, I think we shall see that the opposite is closer to the truth. It is a liberating experience to accept this otherness of God. It opens us to reality, to transcendence, to surprise and to the mystery, not only of God, but of our own being. Time and again Scripture reminds us of this truth. The Psalmist, reflecting on the wonder of God's love, shielding and protecting him no matter where he goes, exclaims:

> Such knowledge is beyond my understanding,
> a height to which my mind cannot attain.
> *Psalm 139:6*

In the book of Ecclesiasticus we read:

Exalt the Lord in your praises
as high as you may – still he surpasses you.
Exert all your strength when you exalt him,
do not grow tired – you will never come to the end.
Who has ever seen him to give a description?
Who can glorify him as he deserves?
Many mysteries remain even greater than these,
for we have seen only a few of his works.
Ecclesiasticus 43:30:36

Paul, writing to the Ephesians, prays they may have strength to grasp the breadth and the length, the height and the depth of the love of Christ, and ends with the paradox, praying that they may know 'the love of Christ which is beyond all knowledge' (Ephesians 3:19). To the Romans he writes: 'How rich are the depths of God – how deep his wisdom and knowledge – and how impossible to penetrate his motives or understand his methods! Who could ever know the mind of the Lord? All that exists comes from him; all is by him and for him' (Romans 11:33-36).

More and more, if I persevere in prayer, I will discover my own smallness and nothingness. But again paradox. In this context of prayer, such discovery will not lead to depression or self-hatred but to a kind of liberation. I will be set free from having to try and impress God and secure his favours. God is all. All is gift. This awareness must be close to that poverty of spirit which Jesus put first on the list of the beatitudes and which opens the door to God's power. Jesus lived in that spirit as Mary his mother did. They lived and moved in this mystery. God is all; we are nothing, but he looks upon us in our lowliness and will do great things through us. Someone has said, 'Poverty of spirit is that place where heaven and earth meet.'

Let us think of other human experiences when we are overwhelmed by something much greater than ourselves, when we become painfully aware of our smallness and weakness. I am thinking of the great eruptions of the powers of nature, like a mighty storm where great electric spears of lightning strike the earth not far away and you know they could next strike where you stand. What are your feelings then? Or imagine you are at sea in a small boat and a hurricane blows up across your path. Or think of yourself at the epicentre of an earthquake, or in Hiroshima the day the bomb fell. At such times we are totally powerless; we are reduced to nothing. In the very worst sense we are annihilated even before we physically vanish, we are reduced to nothing as persons.

But in the awareness of the infinite, transcendent God, who is beyond our comprehension and who is the source of all power, this experience of a sense of annihilation does not happen. The opposite happens. In this encounter we do not lose ourselves but, wonderful to relate, we find ourselves. Because this God reveals himself as love, as accepting love, we find ourselves embraced and held close. He is the God who knows me through and through. (Psalm 139): the One who has always known me (Jeremiah 1:5) and chosen me in love (Ephesians 1:4). We can still feel the sense of total helplessness, but, simultaneously, we feel totally safe. True love does not diminish us or destroy us. It builds us up and recreates us. To be in prayer is to be in the presence of this love. We cannot comprehend the mystery or grasp it or define it. We can only surrender to it and abide in that love. We allow the mystery to possess us and we lose ourselves in it. When we let go in surrender, we may rediscover the truth of the Lord's word, 'Anyone who loses his life for my sake will find it' (Matthew 16:25).

And this finding is meant to be a present experience. God does not ask us to wait till after death to find our life, to discover our true selves. If we lose ourselves in prayer, we will be touched even now by the mystery of God and what we mean to him. In that prayer we will be led by the Spirit to discover not only the beauty and wonder of our own selves but also the beauty and wonder of every other person and indeed the beauty and goodness of all creation. We will become aware that we and all other people and the whole of creation share a common origin in the mystery of God who is love and beauty. We will begin to understand that we are not strangers to each other. We are family. We will be led by the Spirit to pray with the Psalmist, 'For all these mysteries I thank you: for the wonder of myself, for the wonder of your works' (Psalm 139:14). The Spirit will help us to be more ready to notice the goodness in each other and to rejoice in it. Often after a funeral service I have heard people say, 'It's a pity we wait until people are dead to notice and give thanks for their beauty and goodness.' How true!

We finish with a parable. In a certain city, at a busy street crossing, there stood a beggar. Day after day he stood there with his begging bowl held out for alms. He lived on the small offerings dropped daily into his bowl. He lived in poverty and died destitute. When the bits and pieces he left behind were being gathered up for disposal, a city official noticed that the begging bowl had unusual features. He brought it to a friend interested in curios and antiques. The bowl was examined and discovered to be a precious antique of immense value! Are we not like beggars seeking daily scraps of praise and recognition from passers-by, while all the time we are the owners of a precious treasure given to us by that God who has shared with us the mystery of his own being?

21

MYSTERY *v* FUNDAMENTALISM

True prayer should lead us to the God who is mystery. It should lead us away from the childish notion of a God we can define, explain, even control. It should lead us to the childlike notion of God which inspired every moment of the life of Jesus. He believed in a God who was Abba, a loving Father, who was at the centre of life, who held all in his hand and was in control of everything. His being and all the activity flowing from that being was love. Jesus lived out this faith in total trust. All his security was placed in his Father. We can imagine the sincerity with which Jesus prayed the Psalms:

> In God alone there is rest for my soul,
> from him comes my safety;
> with him alone for my rock, my safety,
> my fortress, I can never fall.
> *Psalm 62:1-2*

Let us with great respect and great admiration remind ourselves that this was not easy for Jesus. He was like us in all things but sin. Like us he was tempted. He was tempted in the desert to put his security in miracles and not in his Father's providence. In Gethsemane he is tempted to avoid the consequences of total trust in God and cries out against the chalice of suffering he is invited to drink. But he did not sin. He trusts. His security is in God his Father and he trusts to the bitter end.

We are invited to similar trust but it is very hard for us. When things go badly wrong, we find it nearly impossible to put all our faith in God. We crave security. We fear risk in life. But, at the same time, we say we are people of faith. Now true faith of its very nature involves some kind of 'risk', some kind of 'insecurity'. This is a problem. We too pray with the Psalmist to God, 'You are my rock, my safety, my fortress.' But we also experience distress, doubt and darkness and are tempted to seek security elsewhere. Thus we experience an inner tension. Two conflicting desires are at work within us, to trust completely in an often unpredictable God and to have security and certainty about life – especially the next life – and about salvation.

The understandable desire to resolve this tension and to accommodate both these yearnings in our nature often leads religious people on to a deceptive sidetrack. It is worth noting this danger and being on our guard. A general word used to describe this aberration is 'fundamentalism'. It is a temptation that recurs in every age of religious history and in every creed. I use the word 'temptation' because it attracts us under the guise of good. Fundamentalism professes an ardent faith and a burning zeal for the living God and his place in our lives. But it interprets this God in a way that makes him more predictable and manageable. It keeps faith in God but in a God of its own designing. This is prompted by our craving for security and certainty. Since fundamentalism is a response to feelings of insecurity, it manifests itself strongly in times of change, recession and deprivation. We should not be surprised that recent times have seen a strong, universal upsurge of this phenomenon. Our age offers a receptive climate. The post-Vatican II upheaval in religious thinking; the nuclear threat; the rapid technological development and experimentation without a corresponding growth in moral sensitivity; unemployment; talk of the destruction of the environment – all these foster a strong sense of insecurity and helplessness. More than ever we need some rock to cling to, some fortress where we will feel safe.

The fundamentalist finds this hiding-place in religion, in a relationship with God, but with a God he can cope with, a God he can understand and predict. The fundamentalist will oppose change in religious thinking or any exploration of the mystery of God. It is too threatening. She must interpret God in a predictable and manageable way. But how can the infinite Mystery become more manageable? One way is to equate God with some partial revelation of himself or his wishes. God reveals himself in many ways. For religious people he is revealed in his laws, in the Bible, in a community of believers called the Church. The fundamentalist is always tempted to make a God of law, or of Bible or of Church. The law of God, the word of God, the community of God are all sacred, precious gifts to be loved, but they cannot take the place of God. They must always lead us past themselves, into the mystery of God who is love and in whose image we are created and whose being we are to reveal to all by loving each other. The fundamentalist temptation is to substitute one of these for God himself. They are all more manageable than God himself!

Take law, for example, a favourite 'god' of the fundamentalist of any time or place. We can understand law. It is clear-cut. It tells us what to do, how to please God. If we know what we have to do and we do it, then we are safe before God. We can make sure of salvation. If we keep the law, God must reward us. We can see how this line of thought can lead us far away from the God of Jesus. Indeed, it can destroy the very notion of God altogether. It destroys the sense of mystery. It leaves no room for exploration, revelation, surprise. It is an enemy of real faith. It wants to substitute certainty for trust. It substitutes an idol for the living God and, in a subtle way, it puts us in control of God.

In the gospel, the extreme Pharisees had become such fundamentalists. They could not cope with Jesus and the God he was claiming to reveal and the change of thought he was inviting. How could Jesus be a friend of sinners who broke the law? How could he himself flout respected law and traditions? How could he do all this and claim to do it in the name of God? Jesus was too full of surprise

116

and change for them. They confronted Jesus again and again. In these confrontations Jesus used some very severe words. He accused them bluntly of not knowing God at all, and, even worse, of not having any love for God in their hearts.

> You study the scriptures,
> believing that in them you have eternal life;
> now these same scriptures testify to me,
> and yet you refuse to come to me for life!
> Besides, I know you too well:
> you have no love of God in you.
> *John 5:39-42*

Jesus is saying that it is possible to know the scriptures and keep the law perfectly and still have no love of God in the heart. This is surely a most sobering thought, one which invites us all to reflection.

We can understand why Jesus was so angry with the Pharisees. They were destroying the true image of God his Father. They had put law at the centre instead of love. They portrayed God as a stern judge and not as a loving Saviour. Jesus came to reveal the true God, the God who entered the life of his chosen people as Saviour first and not as lawgiver until later. Before there was any mention of law, God, moved by compassion and love, delivered the chosen people from the slavery of Egypt. Only afterwards was there mention of law when the chosen people accepted the covenant with this saving God and promised to walk with him and keep his wise laws. This they did in a spirit of joy and thanksgiving. In later years, love grew cold but law remained. People accepted the law now, not out of joyful gratitude, but out of fear. It was a way to be on the safe side of this God. People no longer felt they were pleasing to God in themselves. They felt they had to win his favour, to prove themselves. Strict observance of the law was seen as the way to do this. Observance of the law became a condition for receiving God's love. The Pharisees encouraged this attitude, presenting God as the lawgiver who had to be pleased by observance of law, an observance that depended on our own human effort. The way was now open to interpret life's misfortunes and sickness as punishment for failure to keep the law. When the disciples of Jesus see a blind man one day, they instinctively ask, 'Rabbi, who sinned, this man or his parents, for him to have been born blind?' (John 9:2).

The way is now open also for intolerance, bigotry and persecution in the name of religion. The impoverished, narrow and severe fundamentalist idea of God leads to an equally rigid and impoverished idea of the salvation which God offers. This salvation is seen as something static. It is a state which the fundamentalist claims to be able to define, a place where he can arrive even now. In a sense, the fundamentalist cannot be a pilgrim. He claims to have arrived! Then he sets boundaries to this state. He knows who belongs and who is outside. This breeds intolerance. Those considered outside are judged as sinners, as lost, even as enemies of God. They must be forcibly converted or be punished. The line between right and wrong, between good and bad, is clearly drawn. There are no grey areas. There will be no surprises in the fundamentalist kingdom. Surprise is not welcomed by those who crave security. Yet, in his parable of the Last Judgment, Jesus suggests that the kingdom will be full of surprises (Matthew 25:31-46).

The fundamentalist wants the security of certainty and fears the 'insecurity' of faith. But true faith has some darkness, risk, ambiguity and unanswered questions, while at a deep level there is peace and a 'certainty' that the ultimate reality is love, despite so many apparent contradictions. In faith there is simultaneous awareness of my sinfulness and of my being accepted in that state by a beauty and love infinitely transcending myself. This is the beginning of salvation, a process which will develop throughout my life of joy and sorrow, laughter and tears. God is patient with this process, infinitely patient in waiting for us to grow. The Pharisee and his modern fundamentalist counterpart do not have the same patience with their fellows. They want to separate the weeds from the wheat now. God says, 'No, because when you pull out the weeds, you might pull up the wheat with it. Let them both grow till the harvest' (Matthew 13:29). Elsewhere Jesus says his Father is the gardener. Weeding out is best left to the skilled and loving gardener who will have the discerning eye and gentle touch.

Our faith, our religion is not a fortress where we can safely hide and be protected from life's changes, ambiguities and challenges. Our faith is a going forth, a journey, an exodus, a summons to walk with the living, saving God who will be our shield on the journey. Sometimes that journey will take us through the desert when we may wonder if we walk alone or feel that perhaps we are lost. But if we keep trust, our God will provide water and guide our steps in the safe path. We walk with the God of Jesus. This God is mystery, but the mystery is love. The mystery is the loving Father of Jesus who is our Father too.

22

MUSIC AND DANCING

Our faith is not a refuge where we hide from the challenges of life. Our faith invites us to be pilgrims, to journey, to explore. Where do we journey and what country do we explore? You could say we set out somewhat like Abraham, who is our father in faith. All the Lord said to him was 'Leave your country for the land I will show you' (Genesis 12:1). Abraham trusted this word, pulled up his tents and set out for an unknown destination. What land might God show us today? Where does our journey lead? We could describe it as a journey into love, into mystery, into God. Now every journey of exploration involves leaving behind familiar places and situations. This can scare us. As the Galilee song says, 'I'm not sure I want to walk past horizons that I know.' The journey into love can be particularly frightening because love knows no boundaries; it asks everything of us; it invites us even to lose our lives. The one great commandment of love is more demanding than any decalogue or code of law. But the one who calls us forth on the journey promises to be with us. He even describes himself as 'the Way'. If we trust him, we will begin to see that love asks all only because it first gives all. We don't pay enough attention to this. We are asked to love each other unconditionally only because that's how we are loved by God. There is enough love to go round! 'The love of God has been poured into our hearts by the Holy Spirit which has been given us' (Romans 5:5).

Journey and exploration lead us to the unknown and involve risk and a kind of insecurity. This can frighten us. We need not be ashamed to admit this fear. It is a very natural and common human experience. There is nothing wrong in wanting security and feeling fearful about the unknown. But we must not allow this fear to conquer and paralyse us. If this happens, it could lead us to resist all change and growth. It could tempt us to settle down where we are and cease our exploration. It could cut us off from the inexhaustible riches of the mystery of God revealed in Jesus Christ. Jesus himself said that if a seed were to resist the risky process of entering the dark earth and dying there, it could remain alone, a poor dry little object depriving the world of the beauty and fruit it has to offer (John 12:24). In another parable Jesus described how a number of people were given talents by their Lord to use in his service. One of the servants considered his Lord to be a hard master and, fearing to take any risk in using or investing the talent he was given, he buried it in the ground. When the Lord returned from his travels, the servant dug up the talent and brought it to his master. For this he was rebuked (Matthew 25:14-30).

In the last chapter we considered an even worse consequence of giving in to our fear of risk and insecurity. We noted that it could lead to a complete distortion of the image of God and the nature of true religion. Out of desire for security we could create our own 'safe' God, a lawgiver with a set of clear-cut laws. With these we know where we stand. When we keep these laws we are safe and God will reward us. This of course destroys the notion of God as life, mystery, love. He ceases to be the God of gift, of growth and unconditional love. He becomes an employer, a static God out there who pays our wages when we keep his laws and adds an occasional bonus when we put in some overtime by fasting or almsgiving. This kills the living God, the dynamic God of the kingdom present among us, always working with us and for us. It destroys the sovereign freedom of God, because, by observing his laws, we exercise a subtle control over him: he is obliged to reward us. We are thus led away from an open, joyful religion of love, trust and gratitude to a narrow, gloomy, anxious striving for guaranteed salvation.

This 'small' God of our own making is totally alien to the God revealed by Jesus. For him, God is Abba, loving Father, caring and concerned about the smallest details of our lives. Jesus walked joyfully with this God in his own pilgrimage and invites us to do the same. He assures us that this very God, his Father, is our God and Father too. This was the good news he brought us. His greatest joy was to reveal to us the true nature of his Father. One of the most beautiful revelations of the Father given by Jesus is found in the story of the Prodigal Son. Jesus was moved to tell this story when he heard the scribes and Pharisees complaining that he was too friendly with sinners. He was upset at the way these self-righteous men were obscuring his Father's tender mercy. So he gathered the people around him and told them that famous story which began, 'A man had two sons' (Luke 15:11).

In the story, one son, the younger boy, takes his inheritance and moves away from home and his father. He does not move just down the road. He goes far away. He leaves 'for a distant country'. The father loves the boy dearly, but allows him to go. Love takes risks. The father trusts the boy, but the lad cannot cope with the freedom and the money. He 'squanders his money on a life of debauchery'. He ends up lonely, hungry, empty. He has no money and no friends. This is a crucial moment for him but he survives it. He reflects and makes a big decision: 'I will leave this place and go to my father.' What enabled him to make this decision? Clearly there must have been a basic trust in his father, based most likely on some good memories of home. But he still greatly underestimates his father's love. He hopes only to be accepted as a servant. Remember that this story is being told by Jesus who now gives us a precious insight into his Father's heart. Jesus tells us that the father is waiting for the boy, not with stick or lecture but with an embrace, with ring, robe and sandals. Food is prepared, musicians called and a celebration begins. There is music and dancing. Shakespeare warns us not to trust the person who has no music in his soul. Maybe Jesus is saying that surely we can trust a father who enjoys music and dancing.

When reflecting on this story with young people on retreat, I love to say to them, 'Was it not an amazing coincidence that the father of this boy was out at the front of the house on the very day the son returned!' Their response is delightfully the same. 'No! Silly! That means the father was there every day waiting and hoping the son would come. He was always watching because he missed the boy!' In a country village in Ireland many years ago, a young son who had become addicted to gambling left home and went over to England. For a while he wrote back home. But then, silence. Once a week the bus from the city of Dublin passed through that village and every week the boy's mother was at the bus stop in the village square when the bus pulled in. God the Father would understand that mother's heart.

The Prodigal Son is not disinherited. He is received as son and there is celebration, including music and dancing. In a remote village in Zambia lived an old lady called Veronica. She was lame most of her life because of a childhood accident. She greatly missed the village dancing. In recent years her condition worsened and she was confined to bed and unable to move about. On my last visit I found her in low spirits. She felt she was a burden to her relatives who sometimes neglected her. She confessed that she felt less a person and expected to die soon. Then as she went on her face brightened up and she seemed to be young again as she said with great joy and conviction, 'I believe that God will come for me soon and I know that on the day he comes we will dance!' Veronica knew her God. And I thought of words written by Gibran the Prophet: 'When the earth claims your limbs then you shall truly dance.'

But not everyone loves music and dancing! We go back to Jesus and his story. When the Prodigal Son and his father and friends are celebrating in the house, Jesus tells us, 'Now the elder son was out in the fields, and on his way back, as he drew near the house, he could hear music and dancing. Calling one of the servants he asked what it was all about. "Your brother has come", replied the servant, "and your father has killed the calf we had fattened because he has got him back safe and sound." He was angry then and refused to go in' (Luke 15:25-27).

How does the father respond to this situation? He leaves the party and comes out to beg the boy to come in and celebrate for he loves this boy dearly as well. The reply of the elder son, composed by Jesus, remember, reveals a sad and bitter heart and gives us a picture of how religion can go terribly wrong and, instead of bringing joy, love and strength for life's burdens, can bring instead gloom and resentment and can itself become a great burden. The boy answered his father, 'Look, all these years I have slaved for you and never once disobeyed your orders, yet you never offered me so much as a kid for me to celebrate with my friends. But, for this son of yours, when he comes back after swallowing up your property – he and his women – you kill the calf we had been fattening' (Luke 15:28).

These words reveal a sad, bitter and unloving heart. The boy stays at home and works hard but clearly has no joy in the work and no warmth in the relationship with his father. His young brother had moved physically far away from his father, but in a very real sense his heart had not left his father, and when they meet he addresses him as 'Father'. The older boy had not moved physically from home, but what a distance has grown between him and his father. In the dialogue recorded he addresses his father as 'you' and distances himself from his young brother to whom he refers as 'this son of yours'. What resentment is packed into that word 'slaved'. He does not say I 'worked' for you, but I 'slaved'. Fr Donagh O'Shea OP, in his book, *Go Down to the Potter's House*, observes that we only complain about work which we do not enjoy and adds, 'No one would say, I have been singing in the bath for thirty years, what reward shall I have!'

The elder boy sees his father more as a taskmaster than a loving parent. He has kept all the rules and he expects a reward. He has kept the rules by his own effort. He did not seem to feel he needed God's help and now in some way God is beholden to him. In our modern speech he is saying to God, 'You owe me.' He has destroyed the notion of God who gives all as gift. In a sense he does not need God, except as the one who is to reward him. This false understanding of his Father is so sad because it robs the boy of all joy and love.

And this false understanding of his father spoils not only his relationship with his father, but it flows over into his relationship with his young brother. He judges his brother from his own distorted perspective on life and God. In his eyes his brother had failed, he had broken the laws, therefore he should be punished. He has no love, no pity for the boy, only judgment. Notice that it is he and not the father who lists the boy's sins. He cannot be moved by the compassion that stirred the father and sent him running down the road. The elder boy cannot tolerate the idea that there should be a celebration and he won't have anything to do with it. Notice that this boy is really playing God. He is telling us what the father should have done, how God should treat human failure. He kills mercy, gift, love.

If you kill the genuine love of God, at the same time you kill the true love of people. Love is indivisible. Our relationship with each other is intimately bound up with our relationship with God. The way we see and understand God colours the way we see and treat each other. If we expect love from God only as a reward for laws kept, then we will withhold love from each other till law is kept and our standards reached. If I expect reward for law kept, I will expect, even demand, punishment for law broken. The elder boy's attitude to his young brother was a direct consequence of his attitude to his father. If he had had a relationship of love with his father, he would have loved his brother, he would have been running down the road with the old man to welcome his brother, he would have shared his father's joy and would happily have entered the celebration.

When Jesus invented this character for his story, he showed how he understood the complexity of the human heart. This elder brother is a terrible warning. Bishop Helder Camara says, 'I pray incessantly for the conversion of the Prodigal Son's brother. Ever in my ear rings the dread warning. The one has awoken from his life of sin. When will the other awaken from his virtue?' Virtue, which we see as our own achievement, can blind us to the most wonderful quality of God's love, namely that it is a completely free gift which we can never merit. It can also make us intolerant of others and judgmental about human weakness and failure. Thus it frustrates the great command of Jesus that we should forgive and love each other. In some ways this elder boy is the most frightening person in all the gospel stories. At the end of the story, when all are inside celebrating he is outside in the yard by himself, sulking, alone with his bitterness. Is this not a picture of hell worse than any fiery furnace? Let us not try to play God or dictate to God the limits of mercy and love. Let us joyfully confess that God is not man, that his ways are as far above ours as the heavens are above the earth. Let us rejoice that God is unpredictable! He is unpredictable in the most wonderful and consoling way, namely, all we can predict about him is that his mercy, healing and love will always be infinitely greater than we can imagine.

Let us identify with the words of St Paul, a former Pharisee and rigid fundamentalist. 'How rich are the depths of God, how deep his wisdom and knowledge, and how impossible to penetrate his motives or understand his methods. Who could ever know the mind of the Lord?' (Romans 11:33-34). There is only one who knows the mind of God, his Son, Jesus. 'No one knows the Father except the Son and those to whom the Son chooses to reveal him' (Matthew 11:27). Let us be forever grateful that Jesus has revealed his Father to us and revealed him as the Father who is love beyond understanding. What sadness there must have been in that father's heart as he tried to open his elder son's eyes to the true wonder of his identity, 'My son, you are with me always and all I have is yours' (Luke 15:31). This is Jesus' answer to all our fears and anxiety and longing for security: 'Realise who you are, the child of a God who created you simply that you might always be with him and share all that he has. Live not in anxiety and fear. Let there be more music and dancing in the home of your heart. Walk more in joyful expectation and wonder and gratitude.'

23

ALWAYS BE THANKFUL

We have noted that it is part of our human condition to crave security. We are, most of us, prey to anxiety. We would like to be able to foresee and control the future, to guarantee a secure future. True faith invites us to place our security in God. This is not easy. We want to trust God but we fear. We say we trust him, but often we try to keep some control. We try in a subtle way to manipulate God, to oblige him to be on our side. Often our religious practices and our observance of God's law are, in a subtle way, motivated by the hope that this will win his favour and guarantee his blessing and protection. Have you noticed how there can be a sharper edge to our disappointment when a 'good' person meets tragedy and a 'bad' person enjoys prosperity. This is close to a fundamentalist response to God. It is not genuine faith which involves surrendering our security to God and abandoning ourselves in trust to the God of Jesus.

Jesus invites us to see a God of unconditional love, the God who gives all freely and generously because he is love and we belong to him. This God gives all as gift. Jesus invites us to see everything as gift and invites us to a corresponding response of gratitude. This gratitude is a happy, joyful experience and can lead us to true faith and real trust. 'Be happy at all times; pray constantly; and for all things give thanks to God, because this is what God expects you to do in Christ Jesus' (1 Thessalonians 5:17-18). The teaching of Jesus is so simple, so profound. He tells his listeners that the life they have is God's free gift to them. Now if God gave the gift of life, will he not be concerned about the food to nourish that life. 'Surely life means more than food!' (Matthew 6:25). Your Father feeds the birds and clothes the flowers. Are you not worth much more than they? So, do not worry about tomorrow.

If I find it hard to trust, I should ask myself if I have a sense of gratitude. Gratitude suggests that we are aware of a gift received, aware we have something to be thankful for. Do I have this awareness? The more I have it, the more joyfully grateful I will be and the more I will be inclined to trust. Do you think the elder brother in the story of the Prodigal Son had any sense of gratitude? It seems not. He did not think there was anything to be grateful for. He had earned whatever was coming to him from his father. As the sense of gratitude was missing, so was the spirit of joy. He was not a happy person. I find it hard to imagine him laughing. The man was blind to the true reality, blind to the wonder and beauty of his real condition, that everything the father owned was for him. It was all his and he did not have to work for it or earn it. It was all his because his father loved him. 'My son, you are always with me, and all I have is yours' (Luke 15:31). Jesus came to open the eyes of the blind, to open our blind eyes to the incredible, joyful wonder that we belong to God's family and all that God owns is ours. We are not servants or paid hands. We are children and heirs to all God's beauty and glory. 'All I have is yours.' And Thomas Merton adds a beautiful comment, 'Everything is mine, precisely because everything is his. If it could not be mine, he would not even want it for himself.'

Jesus says my life, my self is a gift from God. It is a gift in which God delights and which he hopes I will love and enjoy. Among ourselves, when we take care to choose a gift for a special friend, we hope the friend will appreciate it. A gift touches the heart. It is given because someone cares. It is not a reward for work done. It says someone sees me as special, just because I am and not because of what I do. When I become aware that God has gifted me with life and love and wants to share all he has with me, must I not experience great joy? Jesus experienced great joy simply in being the messenger of this good news. How disappointing for him if we do not seem to receive the gift

129

with a corresponding joy. He says, 'I have told you this so that my own joy may be in you and your joy may be complete' (John 15:11).

Jesus wants to open our eyes to the reality that all is gift. One day he told a story about a farmer who wants to hire workers for his farm (Matthew 20:1-16). At the start of the day he hires men and agrees a fair wage with them. As the day goes on, the farmer finds other men unemployed and he hires them at different times of the day. At the end of the day, he pays them all the same wage. Needless to say, the workers who started work at the beginning of the day complained when they saw the latecomers getting the same pay. When you read this story, try not to get all self-righteous and uptight about the 'unfair' treatment of the early workers. You will miss the whole point of the story and lose the joy and power Jesus wants to communicate. This is not a trade union matter. It is a peep into mystery, into the mystery of God's heart. In fact the early workers were not treated unfairly at all, they got the fair and agreed wage. The point is that the late workers were treated very generously. But the more important point, the very heart of the story, is that we are the late workers! When it comes to loving and serving God, we are the latest of the late workers and yet, despite that, God gives us all. We should not pass over this truth quickly. We should pause and question ourselves and ask, 'Do I really believe this?' We must allow this basic truth to overwhelm us. When we 'see' it, the door is open to a new sense of joy which no one can take from us, a share in Jesus's own joy, and the door is open to a new sense of trust. Surely I could surrender my security to such a God.

The point of this story is that God is generous beyond all our imagining. His generosity is not as ours. He is not a man. He is God. We have earned nothing but we are given everything because that is what God is like, that is what love is like. Let us rejoice in what we have received. Let us rejoice in what others have received. Let the gifts we see in others move us not to envy but to praise of God. God is at the centre of everything. He is at the centre in the sense that he is the source of all being, of everything good, true, beautiful, joyful. And he is at the centre as the God of love, ultimately in control of everything, holding all together and sustaining and directing all in love.

Ask yourself who is at the centre of your life. Is it God or yourself? It is some other person or object? Picture your life as a great circle full of a wide variety of persons, concerns, occupations, dreams, joys, sorrows. If you picture your life as such a great circle, who or what is at the centre? I always used to see myself at the centre. I don't mean that I was a very selfish person, but my life was self-centred in the sense described above, with all that great variety of creatures revolving round *me* in my world and getting their importance from their relationship to me and the way they affected me. Within my circle, God had a place, hopefully the most important place, but he was only one of the many 'objects' within the circle revolving round me. I was like Martha in the gospel, busy about many things. I had not properly realised that only one thing mattered.

Seeing life this way, I was missing the obvious. I was not really living a faith life, not living in trust. The basic, most profound and simple teaching of faith, found in catechism or Bible, is that God is at the centre of everything. And he is there not just as a geometric point in the middle of a great area of space. He is at the centre as the source of all life, beauty, love. If he were not there, all would fall apart and there would be nothing. It was a great blessing for me to become aware of this, that God is at the centre of the circle of my life and that it is he who has given me a place in his life and not the other way round. It now seemed ludicrous even to think of my giving God a place in my life. The proper faith attitude, which sees God at the centre of everything, is the beginning of trust. I live, move and have my being in the circle of God's love. If I really believe this, I should want to cry out in praise and thanksgiving.

How often have we heard people cry out, and have ourselves cried out in time of distress, 'Why me, Lord!'? A true spirit of gratitude should lead us to make this same cry into a prayer of wonder and thanksgiving. What a pity we so seldom count our blessings. We are so quick to notice our sorrows and cry out in complaint. But our lives are full of signs of God's love. Sadly, we take these for granted and fail to give thanks. Have we not got a thousand reasons for crying out in wonder, praise and thanksgiving, 'Why me, Lord!'?

'Why me, Lord!' Why should you have set your heart on me and called me into being? Why give me a mind to know, a body to feel and a heart to love? Why scatter so much beauty in my path to delight my being: moon and stars, rivers and sea, colour, form and perfume of flowers, birdsong, laughter, song and dance, friendship and love – an endless litany inviting my 'Amen' and 'Alleluia'. Why all this for me? Why for me the gift of faith which gives deep rich meaning to my life? Why should I be brought into the secrets and inner mystery of your being by Jesus, and be given your own Holy Spirit to interpret these mysteries which Kings and Prophets longed to see and hear but did not? Why should I, poor Lazarus, be invited to the banquet of the Eucharist, invited to sit at table with God and receive no mere crumbs but the very divine life of the Lord? And why should I be on the invitation list for the eternal heavenly banquet? In our prayer, let us walk more often in the garden of praise, thanksgiving and trust.

Long ago, in a certain city, there lived a king famous for his generosity. In the same city lived Peter, a simple beggar-man. Peter's great dream was to meet the king. He knew that if he could ask an alms from the king he would receive a royal gift. Then one day it was announced that the king would visit the city and Peter felt his dream could come true. The great day came and Peter made sure to be at the front of the excited crowd lining the street. Soon the crowd heard singing and cheering and around the corner came the procession. There were soldiers, courtiers, drummers and dancers and, in the centre, the king riding a fine horse. As the procession drew near, Peter ran from the crowd into the middle of the street. Immediately soldiers rushed to remove him but the king called them back. Then the king stopped his horse, handed the reins to an attendant, dismounted and walked towards Peter. A hush fell on the crowd and then there was a gasp of surprise when the king went down on one knee before Peter, put out his hand and said, 'Peter, what gift will you give your king today?'

Peter was confused by the king's unexpected action. He was also disappointed and angry, but all eyes were on him. He pulled his begging sack from his shoulder, put his hand in among the bits and pieces and felt some grains of corn. He took out one grain and put it in the king's hand. The king showed no displeasure at the small gift. He accepted it gratefully and walked back to his horse. The crowd cheered their gracious king and the procession resumed. Peter, disappointed and sulking, left the celebrations. He made his way home to his small hut, went in and angrily threw his begging sack on the floor. When the sack hit the floor it opened and the contents spilled out. Last to roll out were the grains of corn. As Peter looked, he noticed something shining on the floor. He went over and there among the grains of corn was one large gold nugget. He stared in disbelief and wonder. The silence in the hut was broken by the noise of the celebration in the street and he remembered the king. He had given the king one grain of corn and now he had one nugget of gold. He stood there in deep thought and then said to himself, 'Surely he is a generous king. I wish I had given him more.'

When the great day comes for each of us to stand before our king and when he shows us our heavenly home and says, 'All I have is yours', will we not regret our lack of gratitude and trust and maybe find ourselves echoing the words of Peter the beggarman, 'I wish I had given him more?'

24

TRUST AND COMPLAINT

When we describe life as a great circle full of beauty and wonder, we are not closing our eyes to evil and suffering, we are not being naive and pretending there will be no more sorrow or pain. We recall St Paul's words, 'Be happy at all times: and for all things give thanks to God' (1 Thessalonians 5:17). But Paul, who wrote these words, was a man familiar with a great variety of suffering and he reminds us that every Christian will share in some way in the suffering of our Saviour. Yet, the same Paul invites us always to be thankful, to have that constant attitude of thanksgiving which sees all as gift. We saw how Jesus lived in that joyful, grateful spirit. We looked at stories he told of people who lacked this spirit, who complained about the way they were treated, the early workers in the vineyard, the elder boy in the story of the Prodigal Son. He told these stories to involve us and open our eyes to God's infinite generosity which gives all as gift and not as payment for work done by us.

But this does not mean that we blind ourselves to life's pain. Within that circle of life, besides the wonder and beauty, there is much suffering and sorrow. And we are vulnerable and fragile. Some of life's blows can be hard and our weak flesh will cry out in complaint. Now this 'complaint' is quite different from the grumbling complaint of those who felt they were badly treated, like the early workers or the elder brother. I believe this second kind of complaint, this cry from our wounded and confused human nature, is perfectly compatible with strong faith and trust. Christian faith is not the same as stoicism. I wish to say that people of great faith have often been people of complaint in this other sense, and God can cope with that.

Listen to some complaints from God's friends. 'Is Yahweh

with us, or not?' (Exodus 17:7). This was the complaint of God's chosen and loved ones as they wandered thirsty in the desert after being delivered from the slavery of Egypt. Has not this cry often been repeated in pain by God's people through the years? 'Yahweh has abandoned me, the Lord has forgotten me' (Isaiah 49:14). Thus Isaiah records the complaint of these same people in their misfortune of later years. The Psalmist complains eloquently to Yahweh, 'Lay your scourge aside, I am worn out with the blows you deal me' (Psalm 39:10). What terrible cries come from the heart of that just man Job when God seems oblivious to his suffering. 'May the day perish when I was born, and the night that told of a boy conceived' (Job 3:3). As sorrows pile up on this God-fearing and truly faithful man and God seems not to notice, he prays, 'I cry to you, and you give me no answer; I stand before you, but you take no notice' (Job 30:20). We recognise these cries of this good man who, despite all his suffering, did not abandon trust in God. His cries have found an echo in our hearts in our own dark days. But surely the greatest cry that ever came from a faithful and trusting believer, the cry that must have pierced the heart of God, came from the Beloved Son in whom the Father was so well pleased, 'My God, my God, Why have you deserted me?' (Matthew 27:47). And today we ourselves, who believe and know we are his beloved children, often cry, 'Why me, Lord! Where are you, Lord? Do you care?' God hears our cry and understands our human heart. He does not blame us. Indeed, our cry calls him so close that he suffers with us.

To continue to believe that God is at the centre when suffering comes, is the keenest test of trust. To continue to say all is well and all will be well, when the centre does not seem to hold, when our world is falling apart, this is the highest trust. Here we confess humbly that we often fail. But there was one of our family who did not fail. He is Jesus, the first-born in the family. He is our hope and our power. If we cry out, 'Why me!', then God has only one answer, one word to say, the Word made flesh. In Jesus we have the ultimate answer to our cry of complaint, the perfect, lived example of trust in the Father. The same Jesus who gave that great cry, 'My God, my God, why have you deserted me?', can say almost immediately 'Father, into your hands I commit my spirit.' Perhaps in those moments, the great searing pain in his nailed hands reminds him of Yahweh's answer to his people's complaint long ago:

> For Zion was saying, 'Yahweh has abandoned me,
> the Lord has forgotten me'.
> Does a woman forget her baby at the breast,
> or fail to cherish the son of her womb?
> Yet even if these forget,
> I will never forget you.
>
> See, I have branded you on the palms
> of my hands.
> *Isaiah 49:14-16.*

Jesus can still believe he is the beloved Son and that his Father is there to catch him when he lets go the branch of the tree of the cross. Jesus is saying, 'Despite all appearances and apparent abandonment, my Father is still at the centre, is still in charge of my life. He will bring life out of death because I am his beloved Son.' Trust is a key that opens heaven's floodgates and releases God's power and love into our human person, making us capable of true greatness. Jesus showed us this way, and the story of his followers ever since shows that it is possible for us to follow where Jesus leads.

Ideologies come and go, empires rise and fall, but Jesus remains the same yesterday, today, forever, offering himself to each person, to every age and culture. Should we not go to him when trust becomes difficult? Has he not got a very special care for us who bear his name? We have said that the life of each of us is a gift to us from God. But there is another beautiful truth to be recalled. Each of us is a gift from God the Father to Jesus. Remember Paul's great insight: 'Before the world was made, he chose us in Christ' (Ephesians 1:4). Jesus himself is very aware of this special relationship between himself and his followers. These friends were not casually met. Jesus realises that they are a gift to him from the Father. They belong to the Father who entrusts them to Jesus. He says to the Father, 'They were yours and you gave them to me' (John 17:6), and he prays, 'I want those you have given me to be with me where I am' (v.24). Surely there is a special bond between us and Jesus. He is the vine, we are the branches and the Father is the vinedresser. Jesus wants to bring us safely back to the Father and the joy he has prepared for us. The third Eucharistic prayer says it beautifully: 'May Jesus make us an everlasting gift to you, Father.'

This special bond of friendship between the Lord and ourselves grows and deepens over the years. It should give greater meaning to our lives as the years go on. As we get older, we begin to realise that we will not achieve the great things we dreamed of in youth. We find that we can do less and less. It would be sad if life had less meaning for us because we can do or achieve less. The opposite should be happening. We should begin, even if only dimly, to realise the true greatness to which we are being called and to sense the true fulfilment for which we were created. All our ideas of achievement, all our small dreams start to pale into nothingness as we begin to sense the dream God has for us, the fulfilment he has prepared, 'the things that no eye has seen and no ear has heard, things beyond the mind of man, all that God has prepared for those who love him' (1 Corinthians 2:9). Elsewhere Paul says, 'Though this outer man of ours may be falling into decay, the inner man is renewed day by day' (2 Corinthians 4:16).

The inner person grows as we are drawn more into the fullness of God. Our origin is a person. Our destiny is a person, not some Disneyland in the sky. We are to find the fulfilment of our deepest yearnings in the loving embrace of God. St Augustine expresses it so well. After years of fruitless searching for meaning and happiness in every possible avenue of experience, he at last finds the Lord and cries out, 'O beauty ever ancient, ever new, late have I known thee, late have I loved thee. You have made us for yourself, O Lord, and our hearts are restless till they rest in you.' Finding God, we will find all else in him. If we don't find him, then nothing else can satisfy. Julian of Norwich makes this prayer:

> God, of your goodness, give me yourself,
> for you are sufficient for me.
> I cannot properly ask anything less to be worthy
>   of you.
> If I were to ask less, I should always be in want.
> In you alone do I have all.

God is at the centre drawing us to himself. Love is at the centre inviting us to trust. The heart of faith is the heart. Despite failure, suffering, discouragement, our deepest heart invites us to keep trust and to persevere on our pilgrimage home.

Long ago in India, a very old man was on pilgrimage. The holy place of pilgrimage was situated high up in the mountains. It was winter and the weather was harsh. On his way up the mountain, the old pilgrim stopped at a wayside inn to rest. The innkeeper looked at the old man in wonder. The pilgrim was indeed very old and frail. The innkeeper spoke to him with concern and respect. 'Old man, do you think you should continue your journey? The holy place is far, the mountain is steep and the weather is very harsh. You are old and frail, do you think you will make it to the shrine?' The old pilgrim smiled and answered, 'Well, it's like this. You see, my heart is already at the shrine. So I think it will be easy for the rest of me to follow.'

25

WHEN THE DAY IS DONE

Throughout this book we have constantly spoken of mystery and claimed that mystery is at the heart and centre of each life, of all life. The word 'mystery' is used not to suggest a puzzle which baffles the mind but to suggest wonder and beauty which touch the heart and leave us searching for words to describe our wonder and joy. This is so because mystery has to do with meaning, the deeper meaning of everything. I used to think that 'mystery' as used in religious vocabulary meant obscurity and concealment of meaning or, worse still, absence of meaning. It suggested that a certain part of reality, a certain truth, could not be explained or understood by my intellect and therefore could not be experienced by me. This seemed to say that the only path to experience, to knowing, is the intellect. Truly, our intellect is a beautiful light on life's path, a way of knowing, but it is not the only way, not even the most satisfying or fulfilling way. Scripture speaks of knowing with the heart. 'Everyone who loves, knows God' (1 John 4:7). Mystery invites the intellect to humility, to lose itself in wonder, praise and joy. We humbly accept the surrounding presence of something infinitely greater and more beautiful than our own small self. Our true response to this humble letting-go is not to feel small or threatened but to feel loved, accepted and protected. This inspires joy, a joy akin to that experienced by those early Christians to whom St Peter was writing, 'a joy so glorious that it cannot be described' (1 Peter 1:8).

The old pilgrim in the story related in the last chapter was in touch with mystery. It was the source of his strength to persevere in his climb up the mountain to the holy place. Another word for this mystery is God. Another word for God is love. We exist now because of it.

The mystery deepens when we realise that 'now' is the only time word we can apply to God. He is outside of our time sequence. His name is 'I am' and now is the only time he knows. This means that in some mysterious way we have always been in the mind and heart of God, or, as Julian of Norwich puts it in her own beautiful way, 'God never began to love us.' He has always loved us. We exist now because of his love and are sustained each moment by it. We are that song and God is the singer. God is the tree and we are the branch.

The mystery is 'touched', 'seen', 'known' by the heart rather than by the reason. As the old pilgrim said, his heart had arrived first at the holy place. St John, as we have seen, speaks of this kind of knowing. 'Everyone who loves, knows God. Anyone who fails to love can never have known God' (1 John 4:7-8). Mystery deals with meaning and meaning does not lie on the surface of life. It is the substance underlying the shadow, it is the reality underlying the appearances. The appearances are seen and noticed and we think, discuss and reason about them, but reality is hidden. Reason takes us to the door leading into the garden of reality, of wonder. The heart enters and knows and our whole being rejoices and reason and all our faculties share the joy.

Here is a verse from an old folk hymn:

> Tell me why you are smiling, my son.
> Is there a secret you can tell everyone?
> Do you know more than men that are wise?
> Can you see what's beyond life's disguise
> Through your loving eyes?

The boy in the song is smiling. This young boy shares the same experience as the old pilgrim. He is in touch with the mystery, the reality hiding under 'life's disguise'. The boy can see past the disguises, he can see the underlying reality because he looks at the world 'through loving eyes'.

Love pierces all disguises and sees the beauty underneath and recognises and knows God. When you see through loving eyes and know that the ultimate sustaining reality is love, then you can smile and walk in total trust as Jesus did.

In the song it is a young boy who knows the secret. It should not surprise us that a young boy 'knows more than men that are wise'. Jesus would not be surprised by this. He rejoiced that the inner secret of his Father's being, which is love, has been made known to simple people. 'I bless you, Father, for hiding these things from the learned and the clever and revealing them to mere children' (Luke 10:21). And again he said, 'I tell you that many prophets and kings wanted to see what you see and never saw it: to hear what you hear and never heard it' (Luke 10:24).

The song asks, 'Why are you smiling, my son?' He smiles because he knows a great secret. The first Son to enter the depths of the mystery and know the secret of God's love was Jesus the Beloved Son. Because he knew the secret, he was able to look at life with loving eyes. He could walk in love and joyful trust. He looked with such clear, loving eyes that he could see past all the disguises to the reality underneath. The flowers, the birds, the clouds, the soil, the weeds in the field of wheat, the sheep, the oxen ploughing, the fisherman casting his net, the woman making bread, the vine, the spring of water, the children playing in the market-place, the rabbi poring over books of knowledge new and old – all these spoke to him, even sang to him of a reality greater than themselves, of a beauty beyond imagining, of a protecting, nourishing love sustaining all life.

But above all did this Beloved Son look at people with loving eyes. He was a master at seeing through people's disguises. And what a variety of masks and disguises he encountered. People were disguised as thieves, drunkards, prostitutes, demoniacs, extortioners, atheists. But this man of love was never deceived. He saw the unique beauty and wonder of each person hiding under the mask. He was blind to the labels and price tags we attach to each other. With his loving eyes he could always read the Maker's name and see the infinite value of each person. He wants to open our eyes so that we may see with his loving eyes. He wants us to see each other with a love that will look past all labels, all categories, all disguises, to the wonder and beauty of God's image in each person.

The most baffling disguise worn by reality is suffering. It is the most difficult and disturbing mask worn by the mystery, by love. When life dresses up as death, our faith vision weakens and we can lose sight of beauty and of love. Calvary is God's most difficult hiding-place. But our Saviour's loving eyesight was so strong, he could look at suffering and find his Father there and not lose trust. He could find love under the mask of Calvary and so, even then, he did not stop loving. He forgives those who nail him. He promises the thief he will enter paradise that day. He trusts that his Father is waiting to receive his spirit. He did not expect to fall into the arms of death, but into his Father's arms.

This Father had sent him to share the secret with us, that love is at the centre. The secret is not simply information or knowledge, it is power. When our eyes are opened to find God mysteriously present in suffering and death, we are empowered to follow where Jesus went, to walk with him through suffering all the way to glory. The chorus of the folk hymn quoted above goes like this:

> And if you take my hand my son,
> All will be well
> When the day is done.

Again we apply these words to the first-born Son, Jesus. He took his Father's hand and walked in trust right to the end of the day. It was a long hard day, that Friday on Calvary. But his trust was vindicated and all was well when the day was done. This Son comes to share his victory with